Counted Thread
Embroidery

Counted Thread Embroidery

Jean Kinmond

B. T. Batsford Limited

© J. and P. Coats (UK) Limited 1973
First published 1976
ISBN 0 7134 2663 2

Printed and bound in Great Britain by
Cox and Wyman Limited, Fakenham, Norfolk
for the publishers
B. T. Batsford Limited
4 Fitzhardinge Street
London W1H 0AH

Contents

Counted Thread Embroidery

Embroidery is one of the most ancient skills and is the effect of stitches combining and adapting to pattern and design. Through the ages each generation meets the challenge to the distinct advance in stitch technique and adaptation to the standards of modern design.

Counted thread embroidery requires no special skill. The stitches are worked on canvas or evenweave fabric. A detailed diagram and full working instructions are given for each article.

There are various counted thread techniques many with an historical or geographical background. The following are the most important.

Cross stitch embroidery

Cross stitch embroidery has been consistently popular throughout the centuries. The technique has early beginnings and was found in the peasant embroideries of many European countries. It was used extensively on household articles such as bedcovers, pillows, cushions and tablecloths, as well as on personal wear.

Cross stitch gives unlimited scope to the designer. The stitch itself is basic and simple and the embroiderer enjoys the pleasure obtained from the rhythmic motion of the stitch as the detailed designs and striking patterns come into focus.

Canvas embroidery

Canvas embroidery embraces a number of interesting stitches worked alone or combined in groups. These stitches cover the canvas completely, giving the appearance of fabric. One stitch may be used throughout, for example Gros Point, Petit Point, Cross stitch or upright Gobelin stitch. Gros Point and Petit Point are those most widely used. A selection of suitable stitches can be used together if a richness and contrast of stitch texture is required.

Florentine and Norweave are canvas embroidery techniques.

Florentine embroidery is sometimes known as *Hungarian* Point, *Fianna* or *Flame* stitch. The latter name is derived from the flame-like points which occur frequently in a number of the patterns.

The origin of this style of embroidery is difficult to place, but it is said to have been brought to Italy by a Hungarian who married one of the Medici family in the fifteenth century. It was certainly popular in England during the sixteenth century and again in the reign of Queen Anne.

Originally it was used to cover entire surfaces including stool tops and chairseats, and so added richness of texture and colour to the upholstery.

Norweave embroidery originated in Norway where it is known as *Åkle* embroidery and is popular in the Norwegian homes today. The original design was inspired by traditional bedcovers woven in brightly coloured geometric patterns. All the designs are built up from 'blocks' of stitches, which can vary in number and the length depends upon whether a double-thread or single-thread canvas is used. It is interesting to note that over the years the simple primary colours, used originally, have given way to vivid modern colours and that the designs have progressed from geometric, mosaic style patterns to a graphic style of design using flowers, birds and outdoor scenes as a new source of inspiration. This type of embroidery has a variety of uses: it can enhance a chair or stool; it can be used on covers or cushions to complement chairs, and made into wall hangings or a bell pull to decorate walls.

This attractive and colourful new style of embroidery is quick and easy to do for traditional or modern homes.

Drawn fabric embroidery

Drawn fabric embroidery or Pulled thread work is of peasant origin and is reputed to have originated in the Greek Islands, spreading to Italy, Germany, Belgium, Denmark and England in the seventeenth and eighteenth centuries. As its name implies the lacy effects are created by working certain stitches in such a way that the threads of the fabric are 'drawn' or 'pulled' together to form open work patterns. The stitches are worked by counting the threads of the fabric and the embroidery thread is always pulled firmly with each needle movement, so that spaces are formed between the threads. Although no fabric threads are withdrawn, a certain fragile appearance is achieved and the embroidery remains strong and durable.

Originally the stitches were worked on white or natural coloured linens with matching threads, however, in this book some of the designs have been worked on coloured fabrics with contrasting or matching threads to bring a modern touch to this traditional embroidery.

Spanish blackwork

This form of embroidery was popular in England in the reign of Henry VIII. Many historians believed that it was his wife Catherine of Aragon, a skilful needlewoman, who brought this beautiful style of embroidery with her from Spain. In fact, this embroidery was known in England before her arrival, but due to her influence the interest in it increased and so its name developed. Its popularity continued during the reign of Elizabeth I.

Traditionally, this embroidery was worked on very fine linen using fine black silk thread. The designs were naturalistic in form, incorporating scrolls, flowers, an assortment of leaves, including those of the vine and bunches of grapes. The important feature of this embroidery is the exquisite stitch patterns which fill the various motifs. These patterns are varied in texture and tone, and the appearance of a motif can be altered considerably by the selected filling stitches.

In this book the traditional patterns have been simplified, coloured fabrics introduced, and often coloured threads used, to make embroideries designed for the homes of today.

Lagartera embroidery

Lagartera embroidery was developed in the village of the same name. There the women used to meet in groups to embroider and make their own dresses and household linens. Today it is still the custom for young brides to have a large dowry of this work. Traditionally this type of embroidery was worked on fine linen with brightly coloured threads and the use of geometric motifs suggest a strong Moorish influence. Present day interpretations differ only slightly from the original patterns, but the choice of fabric and thread colours has been adjusted to suit contemporary furnishings.

Fabrics, threads and equipment

All counted thread designs must be worked on an evenweave fabric, tapestry canvas or Binca canvas.

Evenweave fabric

An evenweave fabric should have the same number of warp and weft threads to a specified square.

Tapestry canvas

Canvas embroidery is worked on single or double thread canvas. The best quality canvas is made from what are known as polished threads. These threads are smooth and rounded. Canvas made from this type of thread is firm and does not readily twist out of shape. Purchase the best quality canvas available as this will be the foundation of your work.

Binca canvas

This is an embroidery canvas in which a number of threads are interwoven to form a square. The fabric has nine squares to 1 woven in. (2·5 cm). The designs are suitable for use on similar fabrics with the same number of woven squares to 1 in. (2·5 cm).

Choice of fabric/canvas

The fabrics and canvas used in this book are supplied in different brands and colours throughout the country. In order to help the embroiderer, we first quote the construction of the fabric/canvas and its colour. We also give the name of the leading brand with a description of weight, type and colour, which you can ask for in your local needlework shop. It is most important when working counted thread embroidery that the number of threads to 1 woven inch (2·5 cm) are identical to that given in the working instructions. If this is not so, the size of the embroidery will differ from the original design and it may not fit the given fabric measurements. Should fabric with fewer threads to 1 in. (2·5 cm) be used, then the design would be larger and the cut size of the fabric would have to be adjusted. Similarly, fabric with more threads to 1 in. (2·5 cm) would make the design smaller, in this case it would not be necessary to change the cut size of the fabric.

Embroidery threads

Clarks ⚓ Anchor Stranded Cotton

This is a loosely twisted thread with a lustrous mercerised finish. It can easily be separated and used in one to six strands. For this reason it is extremely versatile, and is suitable for all types of free-style and counted thread embroidery. It is produced in 8-m skeins which are available in White, Black and an extensive range of shades.

Coats ⚓ Anchor Tapisserie Wool

This wool has a wide variety of shades, ranging from the subtle tones of the conventional tapestry shades to the vivid colours suitable for modern embroidery.

Tapisserie wool is moth-resistant and although it is used mainly for canvas work it may be used for free style and counted thread embroidery. When the wool is used on canvas the article should be dry cleaned. If, however, it is used on fabric it can be washed quite safely. Tapisserie wool is available in 15 yds (13·72 m) skeins with a range of 220 fast dyed shades; thirty-five of these shades are produced in 1 oz. hanks, with an additional seven shades supplied only in hanks. The forty-two hanks are known as grounding wools. Each hank contains 90 yds (82·30 m) and can be used when a considerable number of skeins are required and they are most useful when a large area of background has to be covered. Under *Materials*, details are included where grounding wool is most suitable. Sufficient grounding wool for the background should be purchased at the same time, as any slight change in the dye lots might be noticeable in the finished work.

Clarks ⚓ Anchor Pearl Cotton

Anchor Pearl Cotton is a lustrous corded thread particularly suitable for counted thread work. Pearl Cotton, obtainable in two sizes No. 5 and No. 8, is used exclusively in Hardanger embroidery. Both sizes are produced in a 10-gram ball and although the weight of each ball is the same, the quantity of thread on each ball differs considerably. There are approximately 45 m in a ball of No. 5 and 84 m in a ball of No. 8.

Needles

A good quality needle is essential in all counted thread embroidery. Milward 'Gold Seal' tapestry needles with the rounded points which pass through the holes of the fabric/canvas easily, without forcing the threads apart must be used. The needle size is given in the materials required for each article.

Frame

All canvas work should be mounted on a square or oblong wooden frame as some tapestry stitches, particularly Gros Point and Petit Point have a diagonal pull. These frames generally consist of two rollers, each with a piece of tape firmly nailed along its length. One type of frame has slots in the ends of the rollers into which two side laths fit. Each lath has holes at regular intervals at the ends and pegs or screws fit into the holes to keep the frame stretched. There are slight variations to the method of assembly as described above—see illustrations. It is essential that the size of frame should be correct. As a guide, the width measurements of the canvas should fit the tape on the rollers with little adjustment. It is easier to adjust a larger sized frame to many canvas sizes and this is, therefore, more useful. The length of the canvas can be rolled and adjusted accordingly. There are four possible types of frame available.

1 *Tapestry frame* with adjustable wooden sides: available with various lengths of tapes. This frame needs to be supported at each side at a comfortable working height. This leaves both hands free—the right hand to work on top of the frame, the left below. This is explained in more detail in the section on *Stitches*.

2 *Tapestry rotating frame* available with various lengths of tapes. This frame has a depth of 12 in. (30·5 cm) and therefore has the advantage of being easy to carry. However, should the articles to be embroidered be longer than 12 in. (30·5 cm) the lacing will have to be repeated each time the canvas is re-rolled. This frame also needs to be supported at each side when in use.

3 *Tapestry table frame* available with various lengths of tapes. This frame can be placed on a table.

4 *Tapestry floor frame* available with various lengths of tapes. This frame is particularly useful as it stands by itself and can be placed in any suitable position. Your local needlework shop will advise you with regard to the most suitable frame for your purpose.

1

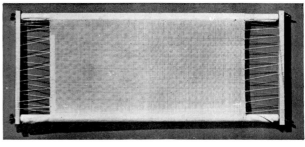

2

3

4

Assembling the canvas on the frame

The canvas should be mounted on any type of frame in the following manner:

1 Mark the centre of the canvas both ways with a line of basting stitches and mark the centre of the rollers with a pencil.

2 Fold down ½ in. (1·3 cm), of the cut edge of the canvas and sew securely to the tape on the rollers which lie at the top and bottom of the frame. If required, turn in the selvedge sides to fit the tapes. The centre pencil marks should be matched to the centre basting stitches on the canvas when sewing the canvas to the tape.

3 Wind the surplus canvas round the rollers, assemble the frame and adjust the screws so that the canvas is stretched taut from top to bottom.

4 The sides of the canvas are now laced round the laths with fine string or four strands of button thread.

Embroidery rings

Some embroideries with areas of closely worked stitches are apt to pucker. In this case an embroidery ring is recommended to help keep the work flat. The ring usually consists of two wooden or metal rings, fitting closely one within the other, so that the fabric may be stretched tightly. These rings can be obtained in various sizes, the most useful type having a small screw on the larger ring for loosening or tightening it. This allows any thickness of fabric to be used. The section of embroidery to be worked is placed over the smaller of the rings, the other ring being pressed down over the fabric on the smaller ring to hold the work taut. If a screw is attached, this should be tightened. The warp and weft threads of the fabric must be straight in the ring.

Special tips

Canvas embroidery

Stretching the canvas

Before the completed embroidery can be made up, it will first require stretching as it may have pulled slightly out of shape. Stretching the canvas can be done professionally. The method outlined could be followed by the embroiderer.

1   Cover a firm board or wooden surface, slightly larger than the completed piece of canvas with clean blotting paper and draw out the shape on the blotting paper 2 in. (5 cm) larger than the embroidery.

2   Pin out the canvas to size, face downwards and if necessary slightly dampen the worked canvas, making sure that the warp and weft threads run at right angles to each other. Secure round all edges of the unworked canvas with drawing pins placed $\frac{1}{4}$ in. (6 mm) apart. The canvas may require careful pulling in order to make it square.

3   It is possible to stretch the threads back to the original form by dampening the back of the tapestry and the surrounding canvas, so loosening the gum or stiffening agent. The gum or stiffening agent then dries and resets the canvas threads. The canvas must then be left for two to three weeks so that the shape becomes permanent.

4   Carefully remove pins.

5   If the canvas has been pulled out of shape very badly, it may be necessary to repeat the above process.

General instructions for working on canvas

Points to be noted for working on single and double thread canvas.

1   Buy all wool at one time, particularly the wool for the background.

2   Use a square or oblong frame, never a circular embroidery frame.

3   Leave 3 in. (7·5 cm) of unworked canvas all round in order to facilitate mounting.

4   Double thread canvas should be trammed when using Gros Point stitch.

5   Make every stitch in two movements.

6   Work to an even tension, not pulling the wool too tightly.

7   Keep the back of the work smooth and free from knots.

8   Work a background area of Gros Point or Petit Point stitch in staggered lengths, not in squared blocks.

9   Never have more than 18 in. (45·7 cm) of Tapisserie Wool in the needle.

Note

When commencing at the centre of a plain area of tapestry worked in trammed Gros Point stitch, make certain that the trammed split stitches are staggered and cross the central line.

Cleaning canvas embroidery

A piece of embroidery worked on canvas must always be dry cleaned as the use of water would soften the canvas.

Marking the centre of canvas or fabric

When the instructions require the centre to be marked 'both ways' use a contrasting thread in the needle and work a line of basting stitches lengthwise and widthwise across the centre. The diagram shows where the lengthwise and widthwise basting stitches appear on a rectangular piece of canvas or fabric.

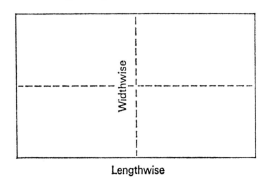

Lengthwise

If the centre line of double thread canvas runs between a pair of narrow threads either lengthwise or widthwise, the black arrows in diagram A indicate the correct positions. Similarly diagram B shows the position for lengthwise or widthwise basting stitches if run along a line of holes.

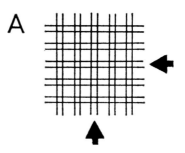

A

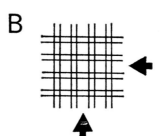

B

Increasing the size of a tapestry kneeler

Should you wish to increase the depth of the sides of a kneeler, this may be done quite easily. As a help, when calculating the amount of extra wool required, we have estimated that 7 yds (6·39 m) of Tapisserie Wool would be required to complete a 2 in. (5 cm) square in trammed Gros Point stitch on ten holes to 1 in. (2·5 cm) canvas.

Layout diagram

The layout diagram shows the complete size of the canvas with dotted lines indicating the basting stitches, also the outline shape of a kneeler. The shaded section shows the area of design given for the kneeler diagrams shown on pages 70 and 72.

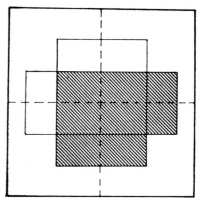

Layout diagram

Making up kneelers

We suggest that the kneelers be made up professionally, but here are simple instructions and a diagram for making up a kneeler.

Join the short ends on the wrong side to form corners and sew close to the embroidery, taking care to match the rows of stitches so that no canvas shows on the right side at the join. Trim canvas at corners and turn to right side. (If using a pad, insert at this stage.) Fold the remaining canvas and baste at the corners as shown in the diagram. Stuff firmly. Turn in the seam allowance on the fabric base to fit kneeler and sew in position.

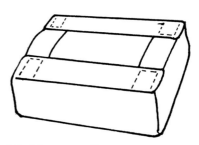

Making up diagram

Tent stitch

Tent stitch is the general name for both Gros Point stitch and Petit Point stitch. The difference is that the first is worked over double thread canvas and the second over single thread canvas. This, of course, makes the latter stitch smaller than the former. If the canvas is correctly stretched on the frame, it is impossible to make the stitch in one movement. When a frame is used, with a little experience, speed and regularity of stitch can be obtained by using both hands.

Method With the right hand on top, insert the needle downwards through the canvas and pull the needle through with the left hand. With the left hand, push the needle upwards through the canvas and pull the needle up and out with the right hand. Gros Point stitch, worked over a laid or trammed thread, has been used in some of the designs. The inclusion of a trammed stitch not only gives better wearing qualities to the finished work, but also gives a richer appearance. The close-up photographs show the appearance of trammed and untrammed Gros Point stitch. All trammed threads and all stitch threads should be of the same colour. The stitch diagram shows the method of laying the thread.

Untrammed stitch

Trammed stitch

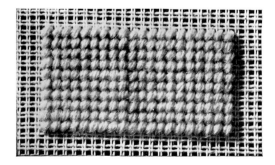

Worked in square blocks

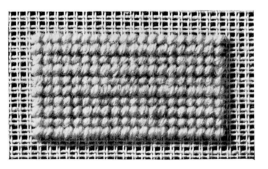

Uneven tension

Norweave

Norweave is worked in blocks of Satin stitch throughout to form an all-over pattern. The blocks consist of four Satin stitches over four threads of single thread canvas (A) or three double Satin stitches over three double threads of double thread canvas (B). The blocks are worked side by side to form horizontal lines of stitchery across the entire canvas (C). This formation must be kept to maintain the characteristics of this style of embroidery. Satin stitch may be worked from right to left or left to right. When worked on canvas, if the canvas is correctly stretched on the frame, it is impossible to make the stitch in one movement, although for the purpose of the diagrams the stitch is shown in this way. With a little experience, speed and regularity of stitch can be obtained by using both hands. The method is as follows: with right hand on top, insert the needle downwards through the canvas and pull the needle through with the left hand. With the left hand, push the needle upwards through the canvas and pull the needle up and out with the right hand. Diagram D shows Satin stitch worked over four threads of single thread canvas and diagram E shows Satin stitch worked twice into each hole over three double threads of double thread canvas to form double Satin stitch.

Diagrams

Counted thread designs are worked on medium weight evenweave fabric or canvas. Each article has a diagram indicating or showing the number of threads over which the design is worked. For some designs each background square of the diagram represents the number of threads over which the stitch is worked. Others show the arrangement of the stitches on the threads of the fabric or canvas. A layout diagram shows the position of the motifs on the fabric. The broken lines indicate the centre basting stitches. The number of threads between the motifs are shown where necessary. To facilitate working, mark the centre of the diagram with a red pencil.

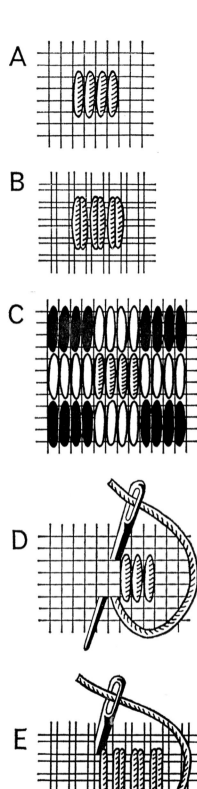

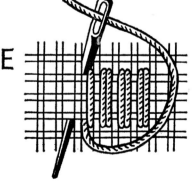

Satin stitch
on single thread canvas

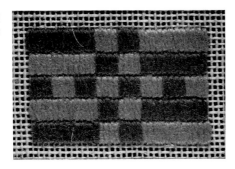

Satin stitch
worked on double
thread canvas

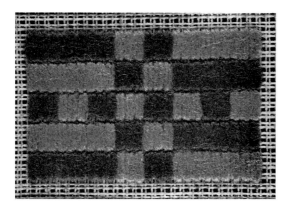

Cutting fabric

Cut the fabric to the measurement given, along the thread of the fabric, then machine stitch or whipstitch the edges to prevent fraying. Each design has sufficient fabric quoted to allow for hems or seams. When trimming the fabric, always trim to the finished size plus hem or seam allowance.

Should fabric with fewer threads to the inch (cm) be used, then the design would be larger and the cut size of the fabric would have to be adjusted. Similarly, fabric with more threads to the inch (cm) would make the design smaller, in this case it would not be necessary to change the cut size of the fabric.

Drawn fabric

Drawn fabric embroidery is worked on medium weight evenweave fabric. To obtain the open, lace-like appearance, the threads of the fabric are pulled firmly with each stitch made. The drawing together of the threads is not shown on the diagrams in order to make the counting of the threads and method of working the stitches easier to follow. With each set of instructions it is clearly stated whether or not a stitch is pulled firmly. It is essential that an embroidery ring be used with this type of embroidery.

Sewing thread recommendation

When making up or finishing articles by hand or by machine, use the multi-purpose sewing thread, Coats *Drima* (Polyester). This thread is fine yet very strong and is obtainable in a wide range of shades. To help obtain smooth and secure stitching on the selected fabric, the equivalent fabrics and needles are as follows: Medium fabrics eg cotton, linen—Machine Needle No. 14 (British) 90 (Continental); No. of stitches to the in. (cm) 10–12 (4–5); Milward Hand Needle No. 7 or 8.

Making up

Making up cushions

Cut the fabric into two equal pieces, then complete embroidery on one piece. Place right sides together and machine stitch three sides, leaving an opening on one side to allow the pad to be inserted easily. Press seams and turn to right side. Insert the pad. Turn in the seam allowance on the open ends and slip-stitch together.

To make up a tapestry cushion

Trim canvas to within 1 in. (2·5 cm) of embroidery. Cut a piece the same size from backing fabric. Place back and front pieces right sides together and sew close to the embroidery, leaving an opening on one side so that the pad may be inserted easily. Turn to right side. Insert pad. Turn in the seam allowance on the open edges and slipstitch together.

Making up tablecloths, runners, lunch mats, etc

Make a hem the desired width all round, mitre the corners and slipstitch (see diagrams and instructions for mitring a corner). Another method of finishing the articles to obtain a flat edge is to face the edges with bias binding (see diagram for method of applying bias binding).

Mitred corner

A mitre is a fold used to achieve smooth shaping at a corner. To mitre a corner of a hem, fold and press the hem; open out the hem and fold the corner inwards on the inner fold line. Cut off the corner, leaving a small seam allowance (*Figure* A). Refold the hem and slipstitch the diagonal line of the mitre in position (*Figure* B).

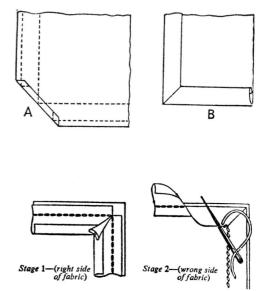

Bias binding

STAGE 1   Open one fold of the binding and lay on fabric edge to edge, right sides together. Machine stitch along the fold mark of binding.

STAGE 2   Turn binding over to wrong side of fabric and stitch invisibly to fabric along the folded edge of binding. For binding, $\frac{1}{4}$ in. (6 mm.) seam allowance beyond the finished size is sufficient.

Stage 1—(right side of fabric)   *Stage 2—(wrong side of fabric)*

WASHING INSTRUCTIONS

Use warm water and pure soap flakes. Wash by squeezing gently. Rinse thoroughly in warm water, squeeze by hand and leave until half-dry. Iron on reverse side while still damp, using a moderately hot iron.

Stitches

The following diagrams give the method of working all the stitches used in the embroideries. The number of threads over which a stitch is worked may differ in each article, but the method of working remains the same. The information relevant to the number of threads over which a stitch is worked is given in the instructions for each separate item shown.

Back stitch
Brick stitch
Chevron stitch
Cross stitch
Fern stitch
Fly stitch
Florentine stitch
Four-sided stitch
Four-sided wave filling stitch
Hem stitch
Mosaic diamond stitch
Petit Point stitch
Pin stitch
Reverse faggot stitch filling
Ringed back stitch
Satin stitch
Satin stitch blocks
Split tramming
Squared edging stitch
Star eyelet
Straight stitch
Straight stitch star
Tent stitch
Trammed Gros Point stitch
Wheatear stitch
Whipped back stitch

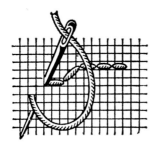

Back stitch

Bring the thread out at the right-hand side. Take a backward stitch over 2 threads (or more if instructed), bringing the needle out 2 threads in front of place where thread first emerged. Continue in this way, always returning the needle in a backward stitch into the same place as previous stitch and emerging 2 (or more) threads in advance.

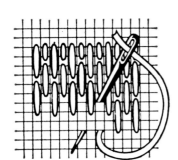

Brick stitch

This stitch is worked in rows alternately from left to right. The first row consists of long and short stitches into which rows of Satin stitches are fitted, thus giving a 'brick' formation. The whole filling must be worked very regularly, keeping an even tension throughout.

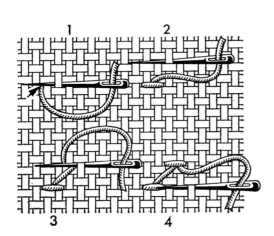

Chevron stitch

1   Bring the thread out at the arrow; insert the needle 2 squares to the right, bring out 1 square to the left.
2   Insert the needle 2 squares up and 2 squares to the right, bring out 1 square to the left.
3   Work as 1.
4   Insert the needle 2 squares down and 2 squares to the right and bring out 1 square to the left. Continue in this way for required length.

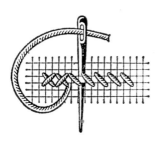

Cross stitch

Bring the thread out at the lower right and take a diagonal stitch to the left over 2 (or as instructed) threads. Continue to end of row making half crosses. On the return journey, complete the cross as shown. The upper stitches of all crosses should lie in the same direction. The Cross stitch may be worked in rows or completed as individual stitches, depending upon the design. On square weave fabric the Cross stitch is worked in the same way, but each cross is over one square of fabric.

Fern stitch

Figure 1. Bring the thread out at arrow and take a stitch 2 threads up and 2 threads to the right, bringing the needle out in the same place where thread first emerged. *Figure 2* Insert the needle 2 threads up and bring out in the same place as previous stitch. *Figure 3* Insert the needle 2 threads to the right and bring out 2 threads down and 4 threads to the left. Continue in this way, all stitches radiating from the centre. *Figure 4* shows the stitches forming an oblique line. *Figure 5* shows stitches used vertically.

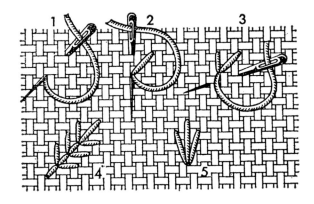

Fly stitch

Figure 1 Bring the thread out at arrow; insert the needle at A (2 squares to the right), bring out at B (1 square down and 1 square to the left) with the thread below the needle point. *Figure 2* Insert the needle at C (1 square under where thread last emerged), fasten off for single Fly stitch or bring the thread out at D in readiness for the next stitch if a row of stitches is required. *Figure 3* shows a row of stitches. *Figure 4* shows the stitch with the tail over 2 squares of fabric.

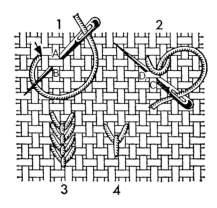

Florentine stitch

This stitch on canvas is used to fill a large area and is then worked in two or more rows of different colours forming an all-over wave pattern. The size of the wave varies, depending upon the number of stitches or the number of threads over which the stitches are worked. On fabric, the stitches are worked in the same way, but do not have to fill the whole area. The diagram shows the method of working the stitch on fabric. When worked on canvas, if the canvas is correctly stretched on the frame, it is impossible to make the stitch in one movement. With a little experience, speed and regularity of stitch can be obtained by using both hands.

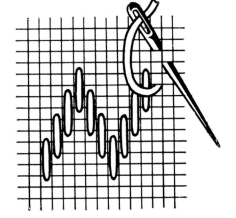

Method

With the right hand on top, insert the needle downwards through the canvas and pull the needle through with the left hand. With the left hand, push the needle upwards through the canvas, and pull the needle up and out with the right hand, following the appropriate diagram and sign key for the design.

Four-sided stitch

This stitch is worked from right to left and can be used as a border or a filling. *Figure 1* Bring the thread through at the arrow; insert the needle at A (4 threads up), bring it through at B (4 threads down and 4 to the left); *Figure 2* Insert at the arrow, bring out at C (4 threads up and 4 threads to the left of A); *Figure 3* Insert again at A and bring out at B. Continue in this way to the end of the row or close the end for a single Four-sided stitch. For Filling stitch: *Figure 4* Turn the fabric round for next and all following rows and work in the same way. Pull all stitches firmly.

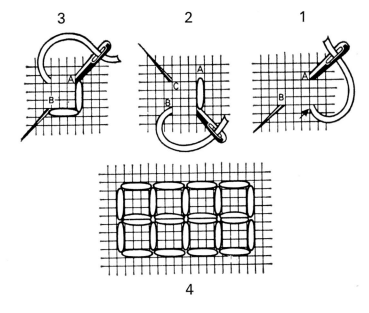

3   2   1

4

Four-sided wave filling stitch

Commence at arrow and work a four-sided stitch in the usual way, bringing the needle out at A. * Insert the needle at B (3 threads up and 4 to the left) and bring out 2 threads up at C, insert at D (3 threads up and 4 to the right); bring out at E and insert at D, bring out at F (4 threads up and 4 to the left), insert at G, bring out at D, insert at G, bring out at E, insert at F * and bring out at G. Work from * to * once more, turn fabric, secure thread on wrong side and work the second row, commencing with a Four-sided stitch.

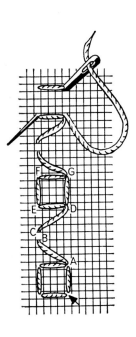

Hemstitch

Measure the required depth of hem plus the turnings and withdraw the number of threads required. Do not withdraw the threads right across the fabric, but only to form a square or rectangle. Cut the threads at the centre and withdraw gradually outwards on each side to within the hem measurement, leaving a sufficient length of thread at the corners in order to darn the ends away invisibly. Turn back the hem to the space of drawn threads, mitre the corners and baste. Bring the working thread out 2 fabric threads down from the space of drawn threads through the folded hem at the right-hand side. Pass the needle behind 2 loose threads, then insert the needle behind the same 2 threads this time bringing the needle out 2 threads down through all folds of the hem in readiness for the next stitch. The diagram shows Hemstitch worked along both sides of the space of drawn threads. This is called Ladder hemstitch.

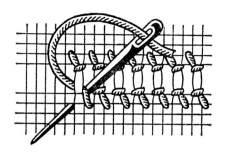

Mosaic diamond

This stitch may be worked from right to left or left to right. The number of threads over which the stitches are worked may vary, depending on the effect desired. *Figure A* shows stitches worked over 2, 3 and 5 fabric threads. *Figure B* shows stitches worked in diamond formation interlocking to form a close filling known as Mosaic diamond.

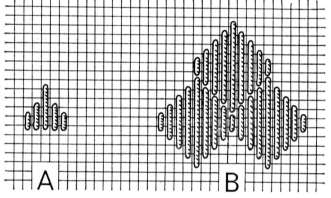

Petit Point stitch

Figure A Bring the thread out on the left-hand side of the fabric on the top part of the first stitch; pass the needle down diagonally over the crossed threads, then under 2 threads, continue in this way to complete the row. *Figure B* The second row is worked from right to left, the needle passing the crossed threads up and over, then under 2 threads. Work backwards and forwards in this way until the design is complete. All stitches should slope in the same direction. The stitches on the reverse side are longer and slope more than on the correct side.

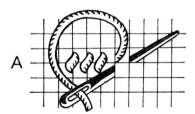

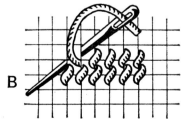

Pin stitch

This stitch is mainly a Drawn Fabric stitch, but it can be used in Drawn Thread embroidery and for outlining applique work. *Figure 1* For a hem edge, bring the thread through the folded hem at A, insert the needle at B and bring out at C; insert once more at B and bring out at C. *Figure 2* Insert again at B, bring out through the folded hem at D. Continue in this way to end of row. Pull all stitches firmly.

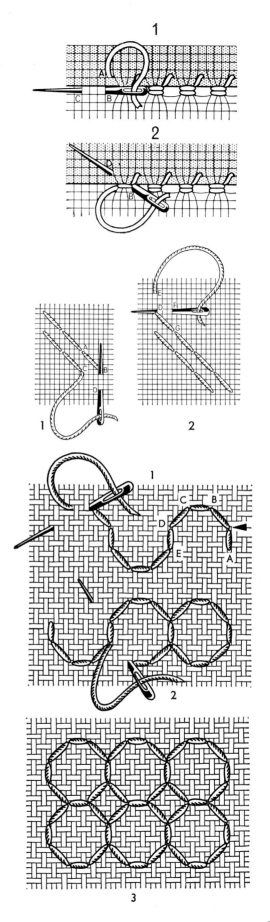

Reversed faggot stitch filling

Figure 1 Bring the thread through at A, insert at B (4 threads to the right and 4 threads down), bring out at C (4 threads to the left), insert at D, bring out at B; continue in this way until there are 5 stitches on each side. When the needle is inserted at D to complete the fifth stitch on the lower line, turn the fabric. *Figure 2* Bring the needle out at E (4 threads up), insert at F (4 threads down and 4 to the right), bring out at D, insert at G and bring out at F; continue in this way to end of row. Turn fabric, work *Figures 1* and *2* alternately to complete section. Pull each stitch firmly.

Ringed back stitch

Figure 1 Bring the thread out at the arrow; insert the needle at A (2 threads down), bring out at B (4 threads up and 2 threads to the left); insert at the arrow, bring out at C (2 threads up and 4 threads to the left); insert at B, bring out at D (2 threads down and 4 threads to the left); insert at C, bring out at E (4 threads down and 2 threads to the left). Continue in this way working half rings, always inserting the needle in a backward stitch into the same place as last stitch and bringing it out 2 threads in advance in the required direction. *Figure 2* Turn the fabric for the second and all other rows and work back in the same way except at the connecting points (as shown) where the needle misses a stitch in order to avoid a double stitch. *Figure 3* shows how the rings connect to form the pattern filling.

Satin stitch

This stitch may be worked from right to left or left to right. The number of threads over which the stitches are worked may vary, depending upon the effect desired.

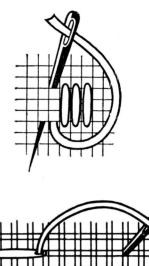

Split trammed stitch

Figure A The Thread is brought through the point where a pair of verticle threads cross a pair of horizontal threads. It is carried along the required distance (no longer than 5 in.– 12·5 cm) and passed through the canvas at a similar crossing of threads. *Figure B* bring the thread through one vertical thread to the left on the same line, through the stitch just made, thus forming a Split stitch. Each trammed stitch must be placed in such a way that the stitches do not start or finish at the same pair of vertical threads. The second stitch diagram shows the Trammed stitch with Gros Point stitch worked over it.

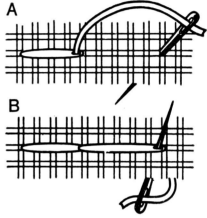

Squared edging stitch

Figure 1 Bring the needle through at the arrow and insert at A (3 threads to the right), bring through at B (3 threads down and 3 threads to the left), insert at arrow and bring through at B in readiness for the next stitch; continue in this way the required number of times; turn corner by inserting needle as shown at C (3 threads to the right), bring out at D (3 threads up); insert again at C and bring out 3 threads to the right; insert once more at C and bring out again 3 threads to the right in readiness for the next stitch. Turn fabric and continue as before. Work in this way on all sides of article. Fold surplus fabric to the wrong side, so that the outer vertical stitch stands out. In order to hold the 2 layers of fabric in position work a second line of stitching as shown in *Figure 2*. *Figure 2* Commence at least 4 vertical stitches down from the corner. Insert the needle on the wrong side of the fabric 3 threads to the right of the outer vertical stitch and bring out at the arrow, insert at A (3 threads up), bring out at arrow and insert again at A; pass the thread diagonally behind the work and bring round at B, insert at arrow and bring out at C in readiness for the next stitch; continue in this way to within 4 vertical stitches from corner. Before bringing the thread round at B, fold back the fabric to form the corner (4 layers of fabric), insert the needle through the third and fourth layer of fabric and bringing through 3 threads from folded edge on wrong side pass the thread diagonally behind the work and bring round at B; continue as before to corner. *Figure 3* Turn fabric as shown; bring out at arrow; insert at A, bring out at arrow, insert at A once more and bring round at B, insert at arrow, bring round at D, insert at arrow and bring out at E; continue as before (see *Figure 2*). Work round article in this way until complete. Trim away surplus fabric on wrong side, close to the double line of stitching. Pull each stitch firmly.

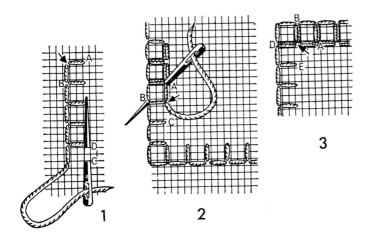

Star eyelet

This eyelet consists of 8 Straight stitches worked over a square of 4 threads, each stitch over 2 threads with 2 threads between stitches at the outer edge and all stitches worked into the same central hole.

Straight stitch

These stitches may be worked singly or in groups and may be horizontal, vertical or oblique as shown in the diagram. They may be worked from right to left or from left to right. The stitches are worked between the squares of the fabric.

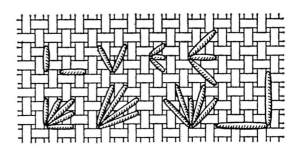

Straight stitch star

These stars are composed of 8 Straight stitches over 2 squares each way of fabric, each stitch is worked over 1 square with 1 square between stitches at outer edge and all stitches radiating from the same central hole.

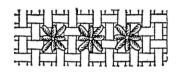

Trammed Gros Point stitch

Figure A Work a Trammed stitch from left to right, then pull the needle through and insert again up and over the crossed threads. *Figure B* Pull the needle through on the lower line 2 double threads (vertical) to the left in readiness for the next stitch.

Diagram C shows the back of correctly worked Gros Point stitch.

It is important that all the designs listed are worked in Trammed Gros Point stitch worked correctly throughout the tapestry, so that an even texture and appearance is obtained.

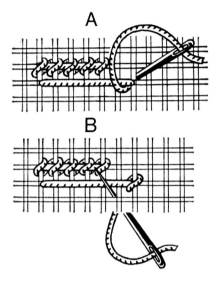

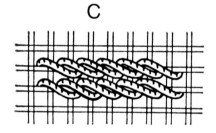

Wheatear stitch

Work 2 Straight stitches at A and B. Bring the thread through at C and pass the needle under the 2 Straight stitches without entering the fabric. Insert the needle at C and bring it through at D in readiness for the next stitch.

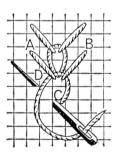

Whipped Back stitch

Work Back stitch first in the usual way, then with another thread in the needle, whip over each Back stitch without entering the background fabric.

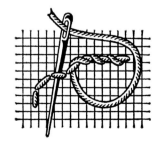

30

Designs and Instructions

Easter Breakfast Set

Materials

Clarks ⚓ Anchor Stranded Cotton: 4 skeins Scarlet **046**; 2 skeins each Cyclamen **088**, Tangerine **0314**, Chestnut **0352**; 1 skein Jade **0188**. Use 3 strands throughout.

½ yd (45·7 cm) white or natural medium weight evenweave fabric, as in illustration, 21 threads to 1 in. (2·5 cm), 59 in. or 54 in. wide (149·7 cm or 137 cm).

1 tea cosy pad approximately 10½ in. (91·4 cm) in height and 15 in. (38 cm) in width at base.

1 egg cosy pad approximately 3 in. (7·5 cm) at base.

1 yd (91·4 cm) matching cord approximately ¼ in. (6 mm) thick for tea cosy.

1 Milward 'Gold Seal' tapestry needle No. 24.

The finished size of each article is approximately:

Traycloth 20 in. — 13½ in. (50·7 cm — 34·3 cm)

Napkin 12½ in. square (31·8 cm)

Tea cosy height 11½ in. (29·3 cm) width at base 16 in. (40·6 cm)

Egg cosy height 3½ in. (8·8 cm) width at base 4 in. (10 cm)

Suitable fabrics: *Penelope* evenweave linen K302 (White). *Beau Lin* evenweave linen (Natural).

Instructions

Cut the following pieces from fabric:

1 piece 21½ in. × 15 in. (54·6 cm × 38 cm) for traycloth.
1 piece 14 in. (35·5 cm) square for napkin.
2 pieces 13½ in. × 17 in. (34·3 cm × 43·2 cm) for tea cosy.
2 pieces 5½ in. × 5 in. (14 cm × 12·7 cm) for egg cosy.

The design is worked throughout in Cross stitch over 2 threads of fabric—approximately 10 stitches to 1 in. (2·5 cm). The diagram gives lower right-hand section of the design as used on the traycloth, with the blank arrows indicating one quarter of the border design. Black arrows marked A on the diagram indicate one quarter of the border design used on the napkin. Black arrow marked B indicates the centre of the design used on the tea cosy. Each background square on the diagram represents two threads of fabric.

Traycloth

Mark large piece of fabric across the centre both ways with a line of basting stitches, which should coincide with the blank arrows on the diagram. With long side facing, commence the embroidery at black arrow on the bird's head 78 threads to the right and 10 threads down from crossed basting stitches and work section as given, following the diagram and sign key. To complete border, work other three quarters to correspond. Press the embroidery on the wrong side. Make up, turning ½ in. (1·3 cm) hem close to embroidery.

Napkin

Mark the piece of fabric for napkin across the centre both ways with a line of basting stitches which should coincide with the black arrows marked A on the diagram. Commence the border at right-hand black arrow (A) 130 threads to the right of crossed basting stitches and work quarter as given. Work other three quarters to correspond. Work right-hand flower motif from diagram in upper left-hand quarter, spacing 10 threads from border. Press the embroidery on the wrong side. Make up, turning ½ in. (1·3 cm) hem close to embroidery.

Tea cosy

On one tea cosy piece of fabric, mark the centre widthwise with a line of basting stitches, which should coincide with the black arrow marked B on the diagram. With long side facing, commence the embroidery at black arrow (B) 1½ in. (3·8 cm.) up from lower edge, and work section to the left of arrow, omitting left-hand flower motif. Continue border to within ½ in. (1·3 cm.) from left-hand side. Work right-hand side in reverse from black arrow B. On back piece, work border only in same way. Press the embroidery on the wrong side. To make up cosy, baste back and front pieces right sides together, taking care to match the border; trim to fit cosy pad, allowing ½ in. (1·3 cm) for seams. Machine stitch, turn back 1 in. (2·5 cm) hem close to embroidery at lower edge and slipstitch. Turn to right side, sew cord in position round seam and insert pad.

Egg cosy

With long side of one egg cosy piece facing, work border design 1½ in. (3·8 cm) from lower edge and to within ½ in. (1·3 cm) from each side. Work right-hand flower motif from diagram centrally 16 threads above border. On back piece, work border only. Press the embroidery on the wrong side. Make up in the same way as tea cosy.

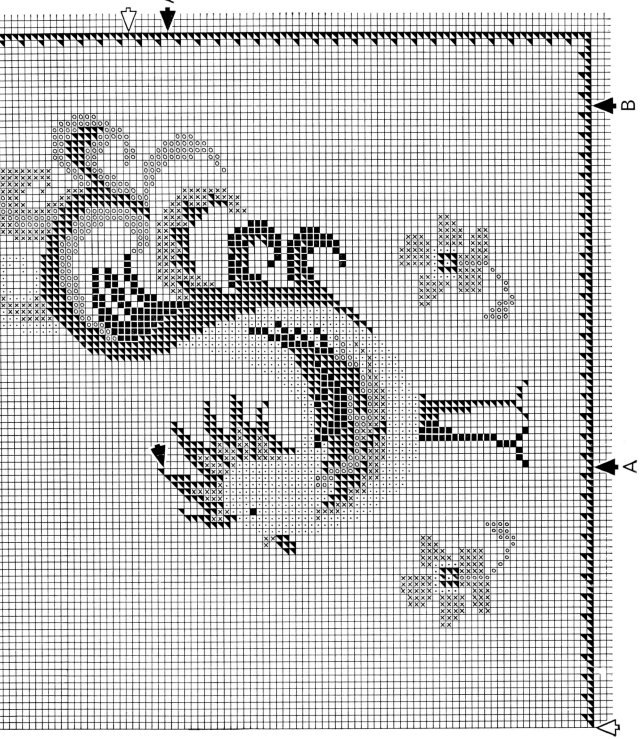

Chairseat

Suitable canvas: *Penelope* double thread tapestry canvas, écru K119.

Materials

Coats ⚓ Anchor Tapisserie wool: 12 skeins **0366**; 6 skeins each **0350**, **0426**; 5 skeins **0381** and 4 skeins **028**.

¾ yd (68·5 cm) double thread tapesty canvas, 27 in. (68·5 cm) wide, 10 holes to 1 in. (2·5 cm)

1 Milward 'Gold Seal' tapestry needle No. 18.

The finished size of the illustrated chairseat is:

Front edge 19 in. (48·2 cm)

Back edge 16 in. (40·6 cm)

Length from front to back edge 19 in. (48·2 cm.)

Instructions

Mark the centre of canvas both ways with a line of basting stitches run between a pair of narrow double threads widthwise and along a line of holes lengthwise (see page 13). Mount the canvas as given in the instructions on page 11. The diagram gives the complete design, centre marked by black arrows which should coincide with the basting stitches. Each background square of the diagram represents one block of 3 double Satin stitches over 3 double threads of canvas. Commence centrally, following diagram and sign key for the embroidery.

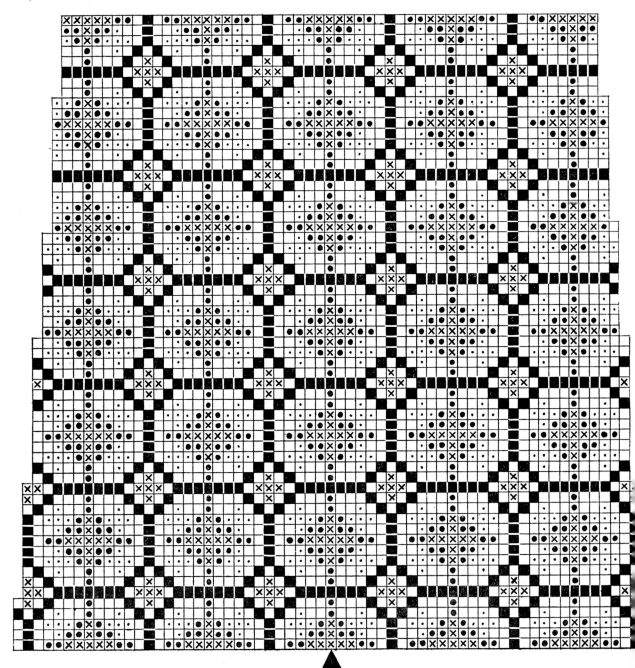

make up

ce the embroidery centrally on the chair
d; fold the canvas back and secure in
sition on the underside with upholstery
ks.

☒	_	028
⊙	_	0350
☐	_	0366
■	_	0381
⊡	_	0426

Jade Chairseat

Materials

Coats ⚓ Anchor Tapisserie Wool: 5 skeins **0167**; 4 skeins each **0186**, **0187**, **0188**, **0189**, **0398**, **0403**; 2 skeins **0402**

$\frac{5}{8}$ yd (57 cm) single thread tapestry canvas, 27 in. (68·5 cm) wide, 18 threads to 1 in. (2·5 cm)

1 Milward 'Gold Seal' tapestry needle No. 8.

The finished size of the chairseat illustrated is:

Front edge   19 in. (48·2 cm)

Back edge   16 in. (40·6 cm)

Length from front to back edge 17½ in. (44·5 cm).

Suitable canvas: *Penelope Petit Point* embroidery canvas K099.

Instructions

Mark the centre of canvas both ways with a line of basting stitches. Mount the canvas as given in the instructions on page 11. The diagram gives a section of the design, centre indicated by blank arrows which should coincide with the basting stitches. The background lines on the diagram represent the threads of the canvas. The layout diagram gives one half of the design, centres marked by broken lines, which should coincide with the basting stitches. Follow the diagram and sign key for the embroidery. Commence the design centrally and work the section given. Complete one half of the design following the layout diagram. Work other half to correspond.

Making up

Place the embroidery centrally on the chair pad; fold the canvas back and secure in position on the underside with upholstery tacks.

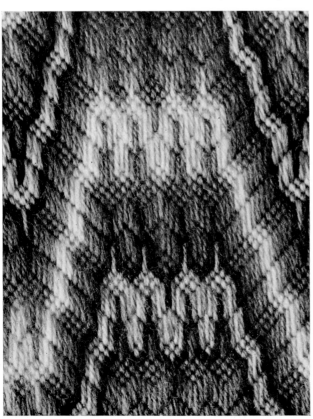

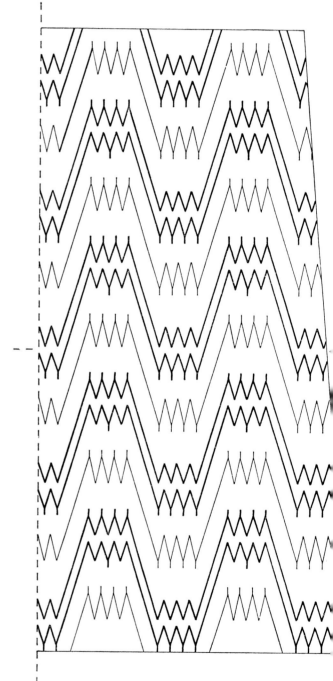

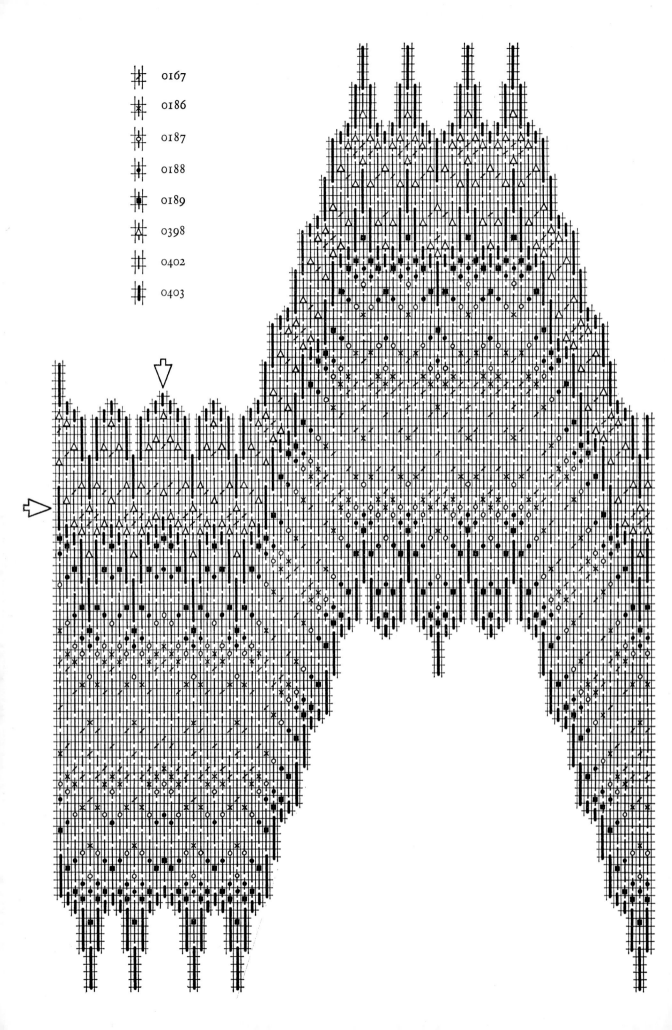

0167
0186
0187
0188
0189
0398
0402
0403

Chairseat

Chairseat

Materials

Coats ⚓ Anchor Tapisserie Wool: 24 skeins or 4 hanks **0899**; 3 skeins **0161**; 2 skeins each **0162, 0163, 0281**; 1 skein each **096, 097, 0217, 0297, 0894, 0895, 0896.**

¾ yd (68·5 cm) double thread tapestry canvas, 27 in. (68·5 cm) wide, 10 holes to 1 in. (2·5 cm)

1 Milward 'Gold Seal' tapestry needle No. 18.

The finished size of the illustrated chairseat is approximately:

Front edge   19 in. (48·2 cm)

Back edge   16½ in. (42 cm)

Length front to back edge 18 in. (45·7 cm)

Suitable canvas: *Penelope* double thread tapestry canvas, Écru K119.

Instructions

Mark the centre of canvas both ways with a line of basting stitches run along a line of holes lengthwise and widthwise (see page 14) Mount the canvas as given in the instructions on page 11. The diagram gives a little more than half of the design, centre marked by blank arrows which should coincide with the basting stitches. Each background square of the diagram represents the double threads of the canvas. Commence the design centrally and work the half given, following diagram and sign key for the embroidery. To complete, work other half in the same way finishing the left-hand edge to correspond.

To make up

Place the embroidery centrally on the chair pad. Fold the canvas back and secure in position on the underside with upholstery tacks.

⊡	—	096	
⊿	—	097	
⊠	—	0161	
⊡	—	0162	
◢	—	0163	Trammed Gros Point Stitch
◣	—	0217	
⊘	—	0281	
⊞	—	0297	
⊡	—	0894	
⊙	—	0895	
◉	—	0896	
☐	—	0899	

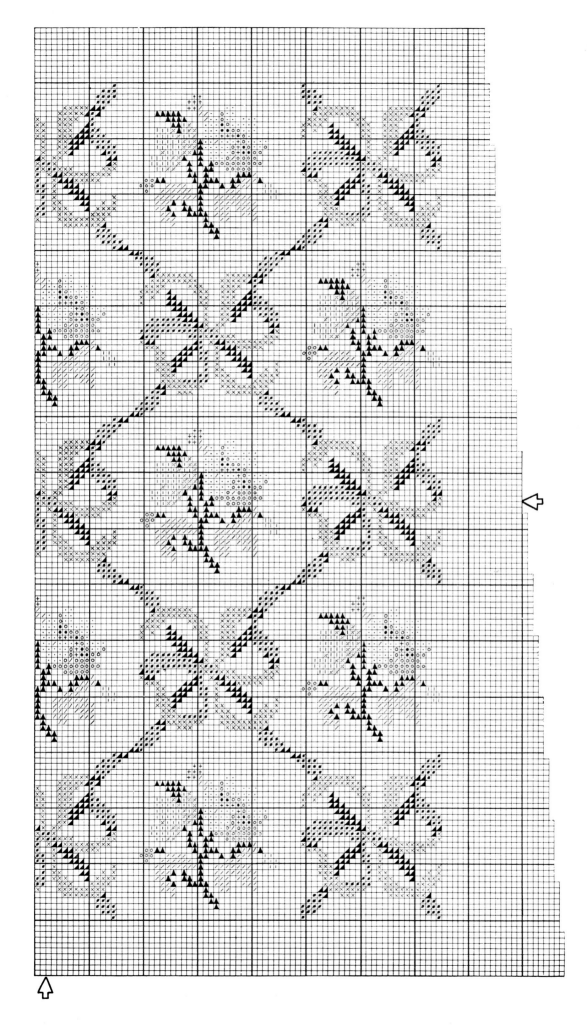

Chairback – *Avila*

Materials

Clarks ⚓ Anchor Stranded Cotton: 5 skeins Cobalt Blue **0134**. Use 3 strands for main embroidery, 2 strands for whipping of Back stitch outlines, or:

Clarks ⚓ Anchor Pearl Cotton No. 8 (10 gram ball): 1 ball **0134**.

$\frac{1}{2}$ yd (45·7 cm) medium weight evenweave fabric, as in illustration, 54 in. (137 cm) wide, 20 threads to 1 in. (2·5 cm) (sufficient for two chairbacks).

1 Milward 'Gold Seal' tapestry needle No. 24.

The finished size of the chairback is $15\frac{1}{2}$ in. × 24 in. (39·4 cm × 61 cm)

Suitable fabric: *Beau Lin* vat dyed evenweave linen (Grey).

Instructions

Cut chairback 18 in. × 27 in. (45·7 cm × 68·5 cm).
Mark the centre of fabric lengthwise with a line of basting stitches. The diagram gives half the design, centre marked by arrow which should coincide with the basting stitches. The diagram also shows the arrangement of the stitches on the threads of the fabric represented by the background lines. Follow the diagram and number key for the design and stitches used. Commence centrally on the basting stitches $3\frac{1}{2}$ in. (8·8 cm) from the lower edge of fabric and work the given half. Repeat in reverse from centre to complete. Continue the border up each side to within $1\frac{3}{4}$ in. (4·4 cm) from top edge then work across top to join as at lower edge. All stitches are worked over 2 threads except the smaller crosses which are worked over 1 thread. Finish with $\frac{3}{4}$ in. (2 cm) hem at sides and top, $1\frac{1}{2}$ in. (3·8 cm) hem at lower edge.

1 Back Stitch
2 Whipped Back Stitch
3 Cross Stitch
4 Back Stitch (Four Square Pattern)
5 Back Stitch (Linked Flower Pattern)

Cushion and
Bell Pull

Cushion and Bell Pull

Materials

Cushion Coats ⚓ Anchor Tapisserie Wool:
5 skeins **0851**; 2 skeins each **0132**, **0188**, **0268**; 1 skein each **0106**, **0123**, **0146**, **0168**, **0187**, **0203**, **0281** and **0423**.

⅜ yd (34·3 cm) single thread tapestry canvas, 23 in. (58·3 cm) wide, 18 threads to 1 in. (2·5 cm).

⅜ yd (34·3 cm) blue velvet or similar medium weight fabric, 36 in. (91·4 cm) wide, for backing.

Bell Pull Coats ⚓ Anchor Tapisserie Wool:
10 skeins **045**; 3 skeins each **0268**, **0333**; 2 skeins each **013**, **065**, **0281**, **0314**; 1 skein each **063**, **099**, **0107**, **0332** and **0423**.

1⅜ yd (1 m 26 cm) single thread tapesty canvas, 27 in. (68·5 cm) wide, 18 threads to 1 in.* (2·5 cm).

¼ yd (23 cm) dark red furnishing satin or similar medium weight fabric, 48 in. (121·7 cm) wide for backing.

Bell Pull attachment to fit each end of embroidered piece.

1 Milward 'Gold Seal' tapestry needle No. 18.

The finished size of each article is approximately:
Cushion 16½ in. × 9 in. (42 cm × 23 cm)
Bell Pull 42½ in. × 6 in. (108 cm × 15·2 cm)

Suitable canvas: *Penelope Petit Point* embroidery canvas KO99.
* It is worth noting that the canvas yardage quoted would allow, if desired, for two cushions to be worked from surplus canvas left over after cutting piece for bell pull. Thread and backing fabric quantities would therefore require to be adjusted (see *Cushion* quantities above).

Instructions

Cushion

Mark the centre of canvas both ways with a line of basting stitches. Mount the canvas as given in the instructions. The diagram gives the complete design, centre marked by black arrows which should coincide with the basting stitches. Each background square of the diagram represents one block of 4 Satin stitches over 4 threads of canvas. Commence the design centrally, following the diagram and appropriate sign key for the embroidery and ignoring the bracketed sections A, B and C which refer to, and are only used when following the bell pull instructions.

To make up

Trim canvas to within 1 in. (2·5 cm) of embroidery. Cut a piece the same size from backing fabric. Place back and front pieces right sides together and sew close to the embroidery, leaving an opening on one side so that the pad may be inserted easily. Turn to right side. Insert pad. Turn in seam allowance on the open edges and slipstitch together.

Bell Pull

Cut 1 piece from canvas 49½ in. × 9 in. (125·5 cm × 22·9 cm). Mark the centre of canvas both ways with a line of basting stitches. Mount the canvas as given in the instructions. The diagram gives the complete design for matching cushion but only the bracketed sections marked A, B and C are to be used for the bell pull and used in conjunction with layout diagram; the black arrows are to be ignored. Each background square of the diagram represents one block of 4 Satin stitches over 4 threads of canvas. The layout diagram gives a little more than one half of the bell pull design, centre marked by black arrows which should coincide with the basting stitches. Commence the design centrally and work the lower half of the bell pull design following the layout diagram for the position of the bracketed section indicated on the diagram and using the appropriate sign key; finish at the bottom with 5 rows worked in 065. To complete the upper half of bell pull, repeat sections AC and AB in that order immediately above centre section AB, finishing off at top with 1 row in 045 and 3 rows in 065.

To make up

Trim canvas to within 1 in. (2·5 cm) of embroidery. Cut a piece from backing fabric the same size as canvas. Place both pieces right sides together and sew down each long side to within 2 in. (5 cm) of narrow end. Turn to right side. Affix bell pull attachments to top and bottom by slipping canvas through slots. Turn in canvas and stitch securely in position Finish off by turning in the backing neatly and slipstitch to canvas.

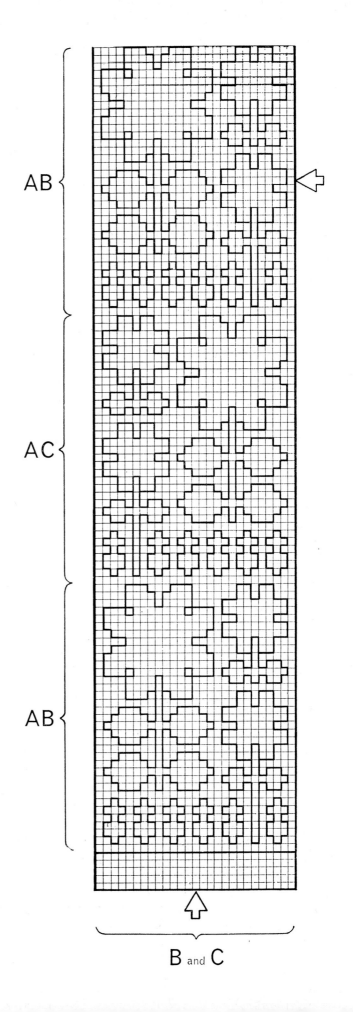

AB

AC

AB

B and C

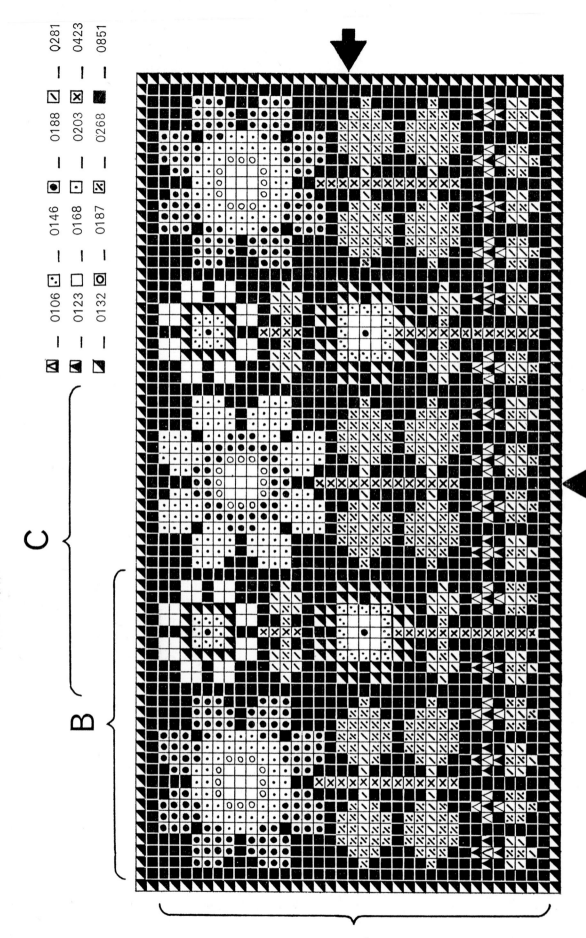

◨	— 0106	⊡ — 0146	⊠ — 0188	— 0281
◩	— 0123	□ — 0168	⊠ — 0203	— 0423
◪	— 0132	⊙ — 0187	⊠ — 0268	— 0851

C

B

A

Cushion

Materials

Coats ⚓ Anchor Tapisserie Wool: 11 skeins
0280; 7 skeins **0403**; 6 skeins **0204**; 3
skeins **0402** and 2 skeins **0268**.

$\frac{5}{8}$ yd (57 cm) single thread tapestry canvas,
27 in. (68·5 cm) wide, 18 threads to 1 in.
(2·5 cm).

$\frac{5}{8}$ yd (57 cm) black velvet or similar medium
weight fabric, 36 in. (91·4 cm) wide, for
backing.

2 yd (1 m 83 cm) black cord, approximately
$\frac{1}{4}$ in. (6 mm) thick for edging.

1 Milward 'Gold Seal' tapestry needle No. 18.

The finished size of the illustrated cushion is
approximately 17 in. (43·2 cm) square.

Suitable fabric: *Penelope Petit Point* embroidery canvas K099.

52

Instructions

Mark the centre of canvas both ways with a line of basting stitches. Mount the canvas as given in the instructions. The diagram gives the complete design, centre marked by black arrows which should coincide with the basting stitches. Each background square of the diagram represents one block of 4 Satin stitches over 4 threads of canvas. Commence the design centrally, following diagram and sign key for the embroidery.

To make up

Trim canvas to within 1 in. (2·5 cm) of embroidery. Cut a piece the same size from backing fabric. Place back and front pieces right sides together and sew close to the embroidery, leaving an opening on one side so that the pad may be inserted easily. Turn to right side. Sew the cord round the seam making a loop at each corner as in illustration. Insert pad. Turn in the seam allowance on the open edges and slipstitch together.

Cushion—*Salamanca*

Materials

Clarks ⚓ Anchor Stranded Cotton: 7 skeins Turkey Red **047**. Use 6 strands throughout, or;

Clarks ⚓ Anchor Pearl Cotton No. 5 (25 metre skein): 2 skeins of the above colour.

1 yd (91·4 cm) cream evenweave fabric, as in close-up, 18 in. (45·7 cm) wide, 16/17 threads to 1 in. (2·5 cm)

1 Milward 'Gold Seal' tapestry needle No. 20.

The finished size of the cushion is 15 in. (38 cm) square.

Suitable fabric: *Glenshee* mercerised fabric quality A.

Instructions

Cut two pieces from fabric 17 in. (43·2 cm) square. Mark the centre across both ways on one piece with a line of basting stitches. The diagram gives a little more than one quarter of the design, the exact quarter marked by arrows which should coincide with the basting stitches. The corner motifs are worked in reverse to each other, the centre motifs are worked in the same direction on each side. The diagram also shows the arrangement of the stitches on the threads of the fabric represented by the background lines. Follow the diagram and number key for the design and stitches used. Commence centrally on the basting stitches counting the threads down

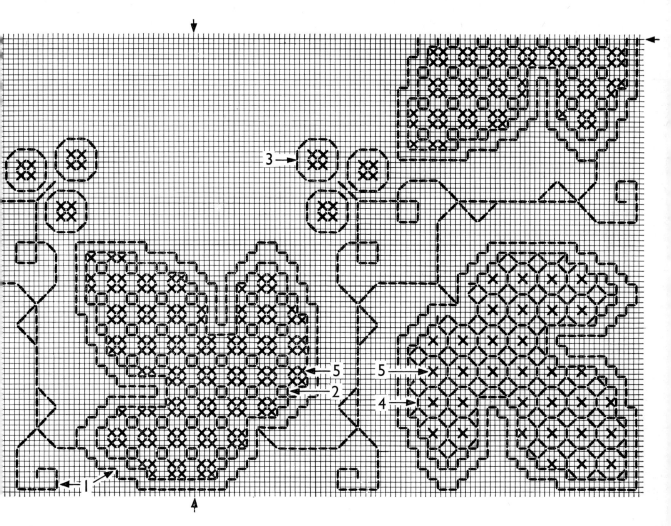

1 Back Stitch
2 Back Stitch Squares
3 Ringed Back Stitch
4 Ringed Back Stitch Pattern
5 Cross Stitch

from the exact centre of fabric (arrow at top centre). Work the section given, then work the other three quarters to correspond. The stitches are all worked over 2 threads. See page 23 for method of working the stitches. Make up cushion.

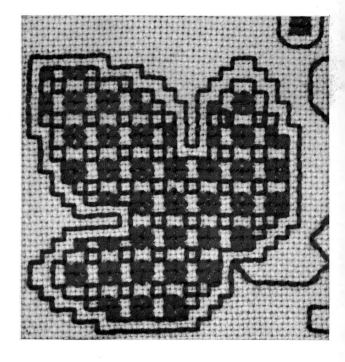

TO18129

Cushion

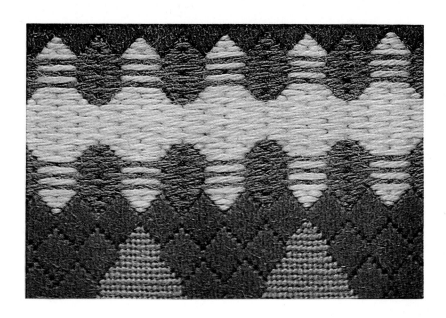

Materials

Coats ⚓ Anchor Tapisserie Wool: 8 skeins each **0105**, **0107**; 2 skeins each **0288** and **0423**.

½ yd (45·7 cm) single thread tapestry canvas, 27 in. (68·5 cm) wide, 18 threads to 1 in. (2·5 cm).

½ yd (45·7 cm.) matching medium weight fabric, 36 in. (91·4 cm) wide, for backing.

1 Milward 'Gold Seal' tapestry needle No. 18.

The finished size of the illustrated cushion is approximately 14 in. × 13 in. (35·5 cm × 33 cm).

Suitable fabric: *Penelope Petit Point* embroidery canvas, K099.

Instructions

Mark the centre of canvas both ways with a line of basting stitches. Mount the canvas as given in the instructions on page 11. The diagram gives a little more than a quarter of the design, centre marked by blank arrows which should coincide with the basting stitches. The background lines on the diagram represent the threads of the canvas. With one long side facing, commence the design centrally and work the quarter given, following diagram and sign key for the embroidery. It will be necessary to work with the side of the frame facing in order to work Brick stitch, as shown on page 23, however, if a table frame or a floor frame is used the Brick stitch will have to be in rows of horizontal stitches, worked alternately from top to bottom. To complete, work other three quarters to correspond.

To make up

Trim canvas to within 1 in. (2·5 cm) of embroidery. Cut a piece the same size from backing fabric. Place back and front pieces right sides together and sew close to the embroidery, leaving an opening on one side so that the pad may be inserted easily. Turn to right side. Insert pad. Turn in seam allowance on the open edges and slipstitch together.

Petit Point
Stitch   — 0105 —

Mosaic
Diamond   — 0107 —

Brick   — 0288 —
Stitch   — 0423 —

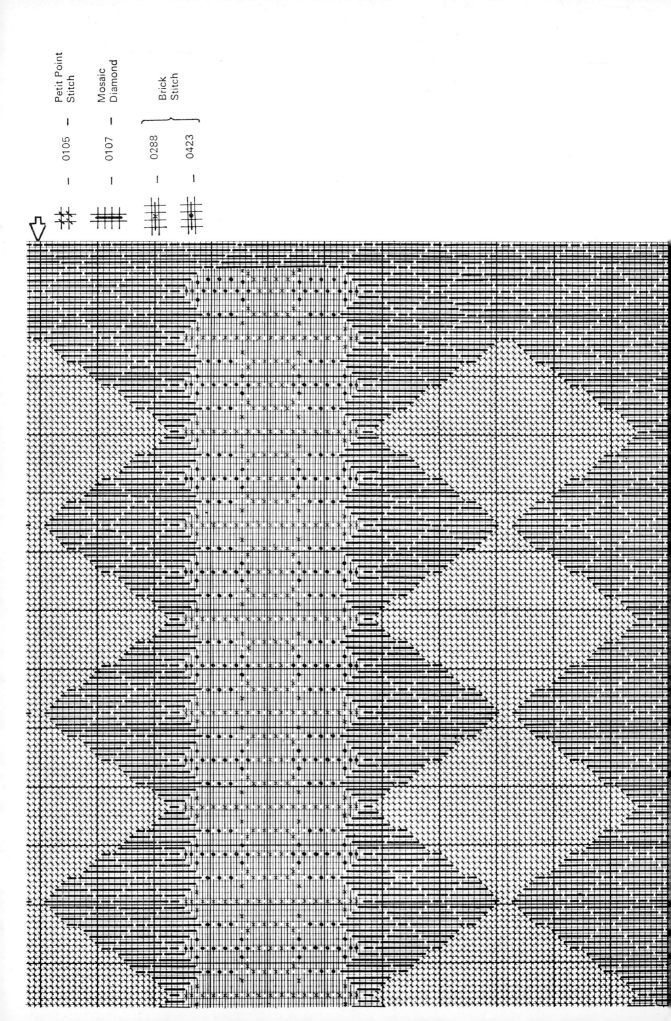

Cushion

Materials

Coats ⚓ Anchor Tapisserie Wool: 4 skeins Apple Green **0205**; 2 skeins each Spring Green **0238** and Muscat Green **0279**.

½ yd (45·7 cm) ivory or cream medium weight square weave cotton fabric, as in illustration. 6 squares to 1 in. (2·5 cm), 42 in. (106·6 cm) wide.

1 Milward 'Gold Seal' tapestry needle No. 18.

The finished size of the cushion is approximately 16 in. (40·6 cm) square.

Suitable fabrics: *Panama* Canvas (Cream). *Castle Erin* Cotton Mesh (Cream).

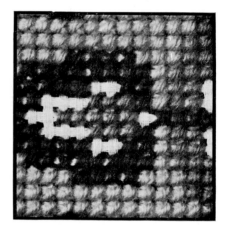

Instructions

Cut two pieces from fabric 18 in. (45·7 cm.) square. Mark the centre of one piece both ways with a line of basting stitches, taking care to have the basting stitches positioned exactly as indicated by blank arrows on the diagram. The Cross stitch is worked over 1 square of fabric, 6 crosses to 1 in. (2·5 cm). The diagram gives a little more than quarter of the design, centre marked by blank arrows which should coincide with the basting stitches. Each background square of the diagram represents 1 square of fabric. Commence the design centrally and work the given quarter, following the diagram and sign key for the embroidery. To complete, work other three-quarters to correspond. Press embroidery on the wrong side.
Make up cushion taking 1 in. (2·5 cm) seams.

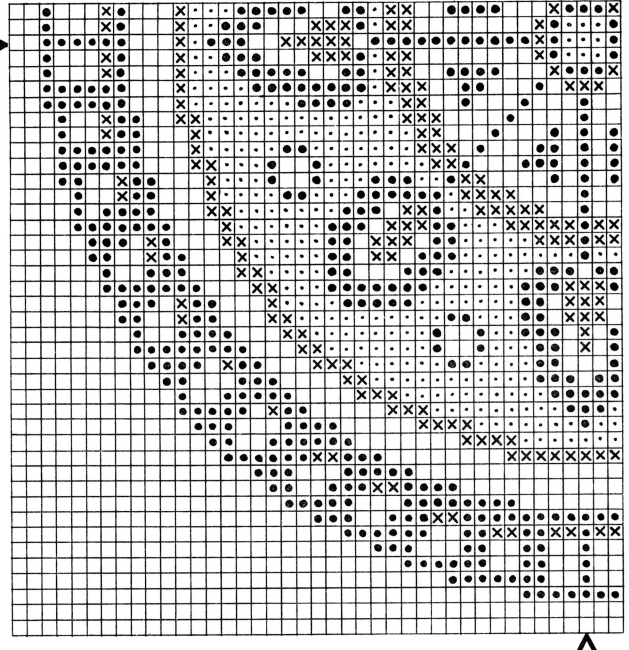

Cushion

Materials

Clarks ⚓ Anchor Stranded Cotton: 5 skeins Almond Green 0261; 3 skeins Jade **0189**; 2 skeins Chestnut **0349**; 1 skein each Electric Blue **0140**, **0143**. Chestnut **0347** and White **0402**. Use 4 strands throughout.

$\frac{5}{8}$ yd (57 cm) beige medium weight evenweave fabric, as in illustration, approximately 21 threads to 1 in. (2·5 cm), 59 in. (149·7 cm) wide.

1 'Lightning' zip fastener, 14 in. (35·5 cm) long

1 Milward 'Gold Seal' tapestry needle No. 24.

The finished size of the cushion is approximately 19$\frac{1}{2}$ in. × 11$\frac{1}{2}$ in. (49·5 cm × 29·3 cm)

Suitable fabric: *Penelope* evenweave linen K303 No. 9 (Beige).

Instructions

This cushion is designed and made up all in one. Cut one piece from fabric 26 in. × 22$\frac{1}{2}$ in. (66 cm × 57 cm). Mark the centre thread widthwise and the centre between 2 threads lengthwise with a line of basting stitches. The Cross stitch is worked over 3 threads of fabric approximately 7 crosses to 1 in. (2·5 cm). The diagram gives a little more than quarter of the design, centre marked by blank arrows which should coincide with the basting stitches, the black arrow indicates the position of fold line for making up the cushion. Each background square of the diagram represents 3 threads of fabric. With short side of fabric facing commence the design 61 threads down and 3 threads to the left of crossed basting stitches and work the given quarter, following diagram and sign key for the embroidery. To complete work other three quarters to correspond. Press embroidery on the wrong side.

Trim fabric to within $\frac{3}{4}$ in. (2 cm) of embroidery on all sides. With right sides together fold fabric in half widthwise. Carefully match up the two rows of 13 crosses and stitch seam close to the embroidery for approximately 3$\frac{1}{2}$ in. (8·8 cm) at each end leaving an opening to insert zip fastener. Press seam open, baste zip in position, turn to right side and stitch. Turn to wrong side, centre zip at back between the two folds (indicated by black arrow on the diagram), leave zip open and stitch across open ends of cushion close to the embroidery. Turn cushion to right side.

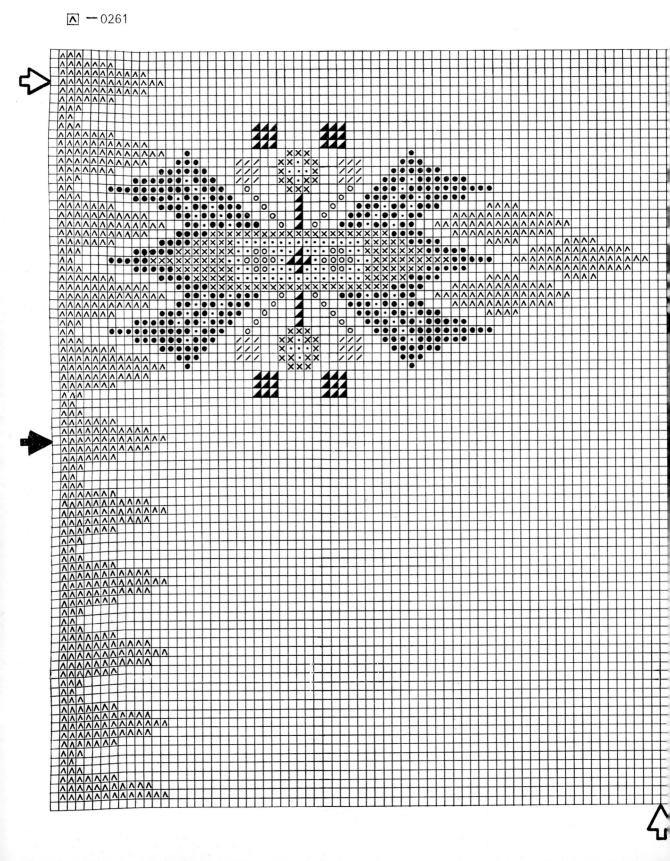

Bolster Cushion and Lampshade

Materials

Bolster cushion

Clarks ⚓ Anchor Stranded Cotton: 6 skeins Black **0403**.

Use 1 strand for all fine lines on diagram, 3 strands for remainder of embroidery.

¾ yd (68·5 cm) white. medium weight evenweave linen, as in illustration, 21 threads to 1 in. (2·5 cm), 59 in. or 54 in. (149·7 cm or 137 cm) wide.

1⅜ yd (125·7 cm) piping cord.

2 black tassels 7 in. (17·8 cm) long.

Suitable fabric: *Penelope* evenweave linen K302 (White).

Lampshade

Clarks ⚓ Anchor Stranded Cotton: 4 skeins Black **0403**.

Use 1 strand for all fine lines on diagram, 3 strands for remainder of embroidery.

$\frac{3}{8}$ yd (34·3 cm) white, medium weight evenweave linen, as given above.

$\frac{3}{8}$ yd (34·3 cm) white bonding parchment, 40 in. (101·4 cm) wide.

2 lampshade rings, 7 in. (17·8 cm) in diameter—one with fitting.

Coats bias binding for rings.

1 tube fabric adhesive.

1 Milward 'Gold Seal' tapestry needle No. 24.

The finished size of the cushion is approximately 18 in. long × 7 in. in diameter (45·7 cm × 17·8 cm)

The finished size of the lampshade is approximately: *height* 10$\frac{1}{2}$ in. (26·7 cm). *diameter* 7 in. (17·8 cm)

Suitable fabrics: *Penelope* evenweave linen K302 (White). *Beau-Lin* evenweave linen (White).

Instructions

Bolster cushion

Cut one piece 26 in. × 20 in. (66 cm × 51 cm) for main section, two pieces 4 in. × 25 in. (10 cm × 64 cm) for ends, two circles 3 in. (7·5 cm) in diameter for buttons. Bias strips required length for covering piping cord. Mark the centre of main section both ways with a line of basting stitches. The diagram gives a section of each border A and B, centres indicated by upper blank arrows (left-hand arrow for lampshade only) which should coincide with the widthwise basting stitches. The diagram also gives the arrangement of the stitches on the threads of the fabric represented by the background lines. Follow the diagram and number key for the design and stitches used. With long side of main section facing, commence border A at blank arrow 70 threads down from crossed basting stitches and work section within bracket; repeat four more times to left-hand side. Work right-hand side to correspond. Turn fabric and commence border B at blank arrow 66 threads down from crossed basting stitches and work section within bracket. Repeat four more times to left-hand side. Work right-hand side to correspond. Press embroidery on wrong side. Trim long sides even and each narrow end to within $\frac{3}{4}$ in. (1·9 cm) from embroidery.

To make up

With right sides of embroidered section together join narrow ends of fabric matching each border section carefully leaving an opening sufficiently wide to enable a pad to be inserted. Turn to right side. Join bias strips, cover piping cord and attach to each end of main section. Join end pieces to form a circle; work a row of small running stitches $\frac{1}{2}$ in. (1·3 cm) from one edge and draw up. Stitch end pieces to main section, joining at piping. Cut two pieces of cardboard 1$\frac{1}{2}$ in. (3·8 cm) in diameter, cover with fabric circles to form buttons. Attach to centre gathering stitches at each end of cushion. Sew tassels to centre of buttons. To complete, insert pad and slip-stitch opening.

Lampshade

Cut a piece 12 in. × 24 in. (30·5 cm × 60·9 cm). Mark the centre both ways with a line of basting stitches. Section A of the diagram gives a section of the design, centre indicated by blank arrows which should coincide with the basting stitches. The diagram also shows the arrangement of the stitches on the threads of the fabric, represented by the background lines. Follow the diagram section A and number key for the design and stitches used. With narrow end of fabric facing, commence the design centrally and work the section within bracket. Work given section from upper centre arrow to complete left half. Work right-hand side to correspond, finishing as shown on right-hand side of section A. Work design once more above and below completed border, leaving 75 threads between.

To make up

Bind rings tightly overlapping edges of tape. Cut bonding parchment 10$\frac{1}{2}$ in. × 23 in. (26·7 cm × 58·3 cm). Place on a flat surface, shiny side up; place the wrong side of fabric centrally on to parchment with fabric extending $\frac{1}{2}$ in. (1·3 cm) at one narrow end and even at the other. Hold in position with paper clips or weights; pass a moderately hot iron over the fabric to enable the parchment to adhere. Turn back $\frac{1}{2}$ in. (1·3 cm) margin and stick to parchment with adhesive. Pin fabric-covered parchment in position around rings. Using small stitches, sew to top ring starting with unfinished short end and stopping about 2 in. (50 cm) from other end; stitch bottom ring in position in same way; tuck the unfinished end beneath finished end and stick in position. Finish sewing at top and bottom edges.

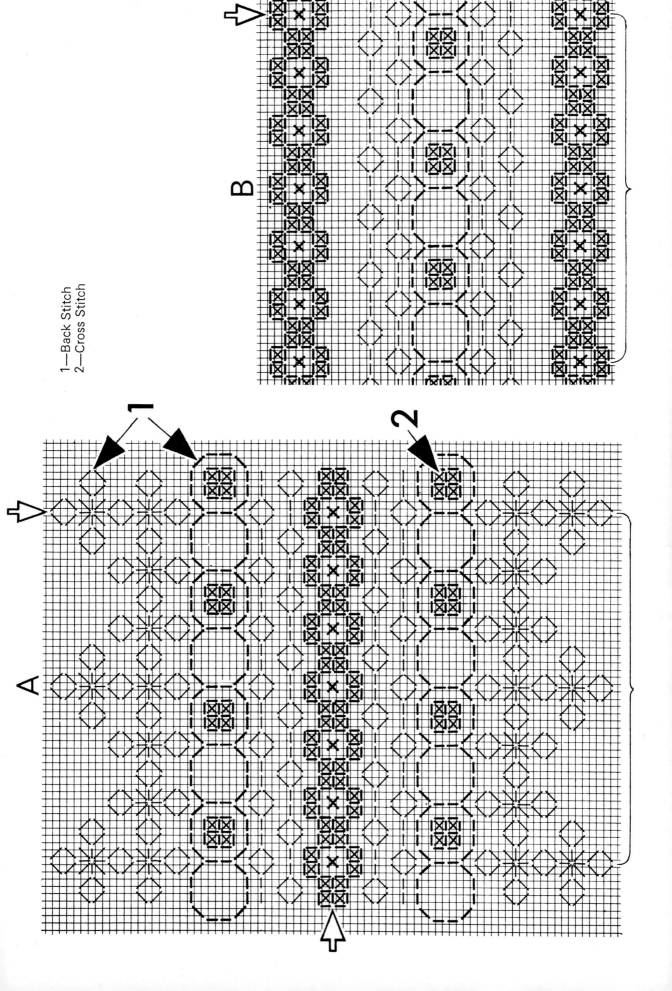

1—Back Stitch
2—Cross Stitch

A

B

Kneeler—*Coventry*

Kneeler—*Coventry*

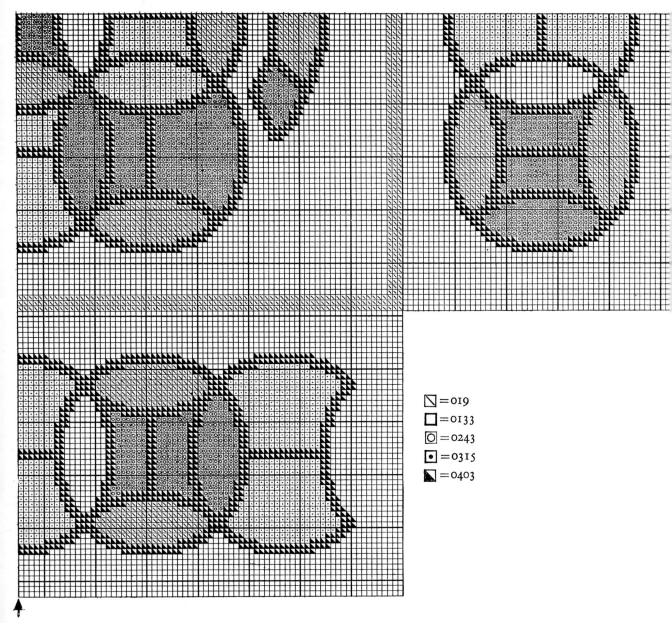

◸	= 019
☐	= 0133
⊙	= 0243
⊡	= 0315
◣	= 0403

Kneeler—*Coventry*

Materials

Coats ⚓ Anchor Tapisserie Wool: 22 skeins **0133**; 2 hanks or 12 skeins **0403**; 7 skeins **0315**; 6 skeins **019** and **0243**.

$\frac{7}{8}$ yd (80 cm) double thread tapestry canvas, 10 holes to 1 in. (2·5 cm), 36 in. (91·4 cm) wide, or 1 yd 27 in. (159·9 cm) wide.

1 Milward 'Gold Seal' tapestry needle No. 18.

Optional (see 'Making up' page 14).
Piece of furnishing velvet to match, or tailor's linen 14 in. × 17 in. (35·5 cm × 43·2 cm) for base.

Filling   Foam chips, Kapok or pad to fit.

The finished size of the kneeler is approximately: *Top* 12 in. × 15 in. (30·5 cm × 38 cm); *depth* 5$\frac{1}{2}$ in. (14 cm)

Suitable canvas: *Penelope* double thread tapestry canvas écru K**119**

Instructions

The centre of the canvas should already be marked (see 'Assembling the Canvas on the Frame' page 11). Each background square on the diagram represents the double thread of the canvas. The diagram above gives the right-hand quarter of the design, centre indicated by the black arrows, which should coincide with the basting stitches. Follow the above diagram and sign key for the embroidery. Commence centrally and work the given quarter. Work in reverse from centre arrow to complete one half. Work other half to correspond.

When a 27 in. (68·5 cm) wide canvas is used, this design should be turned so that it is placed centrally on the piece of canvas with the narrow end between the two selvedges.

The Gros Point stitch should still be worked as instructed, i.e. the trammed stitch lying between the selvedges. It should, however, be noted that when a design is turned in this manner, the stitch is viewed from the side of the kneeler rather than from the front of the kneeler.

Kneeler—*Wells*

Materials

Coats ⚓ Anchor Tapisserie Wool: 22 skeins **0860**; 14 skeins **0402**; 1 hank or 6 skeins **0862**; 4 skeins **0309**; 1 skein each **0264**, **0270** and **0848**.

¾ yd (68·5 cm) double thread tapestry canvas, 10 holes to 1 in. (2·5 cm), 27 in. (68·5 cm) wide.

1 Milward 'Gold Seal' tapestry needle No. 18.

Optional (see 'Making up' page 14).
Piece of furnishing velvet to match, or tailor's linen 14 in. × 17 in. (35·5 cm × 43·2 cm)

Filling   Foam chips, Kapok or pad to fit.

The finished size of the kneeler is approximately: *Top* 12 in. × 15 in. (30·5 cm × 38 cm); *depth* 3½ in. (8·8 cm)

Suitable canvas: *Penelope* double thread tapestry canvas écru **K119**

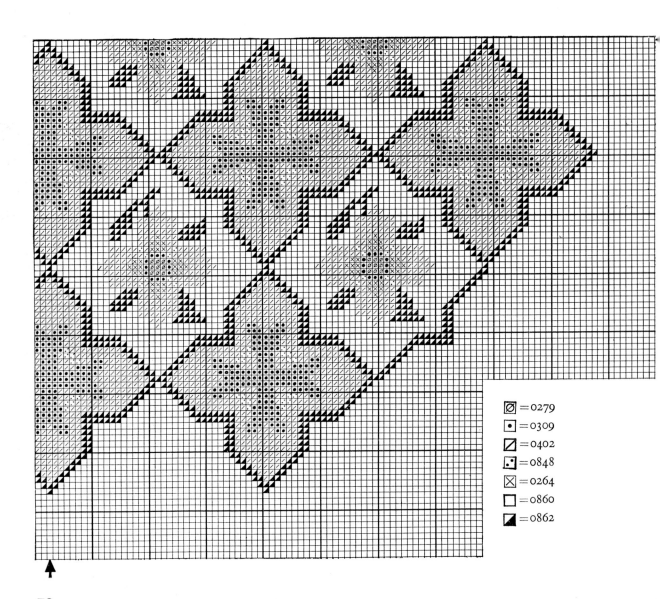

⊘ = 0279
• = 0309
⊿ = 0402
⦂ = 0848
⊠ = 0264
☐ = 0860
◪ = 0862

Instructions

The centre of the canvas should already be marked (see 'Assembling the Canvas on the Frame', page 11). Each background square on the diagram represents the double thread of the canvas. The diagram gives the right-hand quarter of the design, centre indicated by black arrows, which should coincide with the basting stitches. Follow diagram and sign key for the embroidery. Commence centrally and work the given quarter. Repeat on other three quarters to correspond.

Kneeler

	0347	0366	0397	0402
	—	—	—	—
	⊠	⊡	◉	☐

	0163	0265	0266	0268
	—	—	—	—
	■	◣	⊠	⊙

Materials

Coats ⚓ Anchor Tapisserie Wool: 17 skeins
 0163; 8 skeins **0366**; 5 skeins **0402**; 2
 skeins **0397**; 1 skein each **0265**, **0266**,
 0268 and **0347**.

$\frac{7}{8}$ yd (80 cm) single thread tapestry canvas,
 27 in. (68·5 cm) wide, 18 threads to 1 in.
 (2·5 cm.).

1 Milward 'Gold Seal' tapestry needle No. 18.

Optional (see 'Making up' page 14).

Piece of matching furnishing fabric or velvet
 14 in. × 18 in. (35·5 cm × 45·7 cm) for
 base.

Filling Foam chips, Kapok or pad to fit.

The finished size of the kneeler is approximately: *Top* 11½ in. × 16 in. (29·3 cm ×
 40·6 cm); *depth* 4 in. (10 cm)

Suitable canvas: *Penelope Petit Point* embroidery canvas, K099.

Instructions

Mark the centre of canvas both ways with a
line of basting stitches. Mount the canvas as
described on page 11, but have the selvedges to the tapes instead of the cut edges,
as the length of this design exceeds the width
of the canvas; turn in the surplus canvas at
each side. The stitches are worked in the
same way horizontally across the entire canvas. The diagram gives the complete design
for the top, one narrow side and one long
side, centre marked by black arrows which
should coincide with the basting stitches.
Each background square of the diagram
represents one block of 4 Satin stitches over
4 threads of canvas. Commence the design
centrally, following the diagram and sign key
for the embroidery and work the top and side
sections. Work each side once more in required position.

Table mats—*Malaga*

Materials

Clarks ⚓ Anchor Stranded Cotton: 5 skeins Moss Green **0268** and 2 skeins Black **0403**. Use 3 strands throughout, or;

Clarks ⚓ Anchor Pearl Cotton No. 8 (10 gram ball): 1 ball each of the above colours.

$\frac{3}{8}$ yd (34·3 cm) green medium weight even-weave fabric, as in illustration, 59 in. (149·7 cm) or 54 in. (137 cm) wide, 21 threads to 1 in. (2·5 cm).

1 Milward 'Gold Seal' tapestry needle No. 24.

The finished sizes of the mats: *centre mat* 12 in. × 16 in. (30·5 cm × 40·6 cm), *place mats* 10½ in. × 16 in. 26·7 cm × 40·6 cm)

Suitable fabrics: *Penelope* evenweave linen K303 No. 21 (Ripple Green). *Beau-Lin* vat dyed evenweave linen (Green).

Instructions

Cut centre mat 13½ in. × 17½ in. (34·3 cm × 44·5 cm) and two place mats 12 in. × 17½ in. (30·5 cm × 44·5 cm). Mark the centre both ways with a line of basting stitches. The diagram gives one-quarter of the centre mat, centres marked by single arrows which should coincide with the basting stitches. The double arrows give the centre width-wise of the place mats and should also coincide with the basting stitches. The large motifs are worked on one long side of small mats and both sides of centre mat. The diagram also shows the arrangement of the stitches on the threads of the fabric represented by the background lines. Follow the diagram and number key for the design and stitches used. Commence centre mat on the basting stitches at top left arrow on diagram, 40 threads from the exact centre of fabric. Work the given quarter then repeat in reverse from arrows for the other three quarters. On place mats, commence centrally in same way 24 threads from the exact centre. Work the given section then repeat in reverse from left-hand arrows to complete half the narrow border and five large motifs. Now repeat the narrow border only from centre to complete the design. All stitches are worked over 2 threads of fabric. See page 23 for method of working the stitches. Finish with $\frac{3}{4}$ in. (2 cm) hems.

1—**0268** ⎱ Back Stitch
2—**0403** ⎰
3—**0268** Straight Stitch
4—**0268** Star Eyelet
5—**0403** Cross Stitch
6—**0268** Back Stitch (Medallion Pattern)

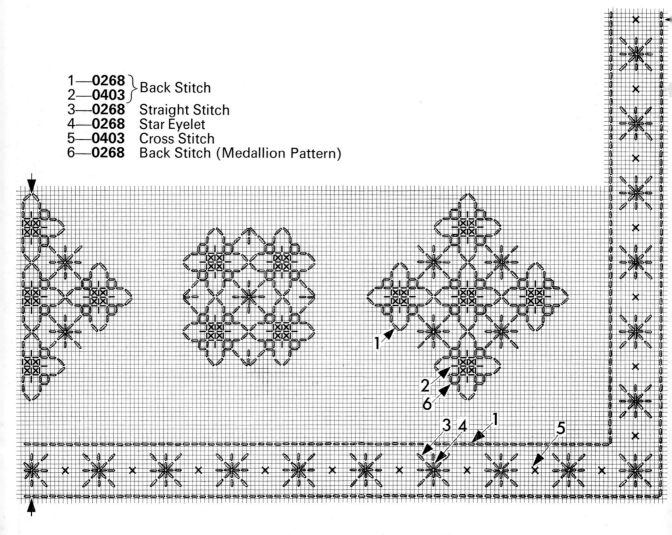

Luncheon set

Materials

Clarks ⚓ Anchor Stranded Cotton: 4 skeins Black **0403**. Use 3 strands throughout.

½ yd (45·7 cm) red, medium weight even-weave fabric, as in illustration, 21 threads to 1 in. (2·5 cm), 59 in. (149·7 cm) wide.

1 Milward 'Gold Seal' tapestry needle No. 24.

The finished size of each small mat is approximately 11 in. × 16 in. (28 cm × 40·6 cm) and the runner 11 in. × 31 in. (28 cm × 78·7 cm)

Suitable fabric: *Penelope* evenweave linen K303 shade No. 50 (Procion Red).

Instructions

Cut two pieces from fabric 13 in. × 18 in. (33 cm × 45·7 cm) for small mats and one piece 13 in. × 33 in (33 cm. × 83·8 cm) for runner. Mark the centre both ways on each piece of fabric with a line of basting stitches. The diagram gives the three motifs and a little more than half the border design and corner turning for the small mats, centre lengthwise basting stitches indicated by blank arrow. The diagram also shows the arrangement of the stitches on the threads of the fabric represented by the background lines. The layout diagram shows the placing of the border and the motifs on a little more than a quarter of the runner, centre indicated by broken lines which should coincide with the basting stitches. The numerals give the number of threads between the motif and the border. Follow the diagram and number key for the design and stitches used. With long side of small piece of fabric facing, commence the design on the lengthwise basting stitches 101 threads to the left of the crossed basting stitches and work the section given on the diagram. Repeat given section in same way on to the right-hand side of the fabric reversing corner turning. Complete the border by repeating the section within the bracket 8 times on each long side and 5 times on each narrow end, plus corner turnings. With narrow end of long piece of fabric facing, commence centrally on widthwise basting stitches 107 threads to the left of the crossed basting stitches and work the border design and motifs following layout diagram. Turn fabric and work on other narrow end in same way. Complete border pattern. The section within the bracket on the diagram is repeated 17 times on each long side and 5 times on each narrow end, plus corner turnings. Trim margins even. Press the embroidery on the wrong side. Make-up taking ½ in. (1·3 cm.) hems, 4 fabric threads are left between border and finished edge.

1   Back Stitch
2   Four-sided Stitch
3   Straight Stitch
4   Wheatear Stitch
5   Fern Stitch

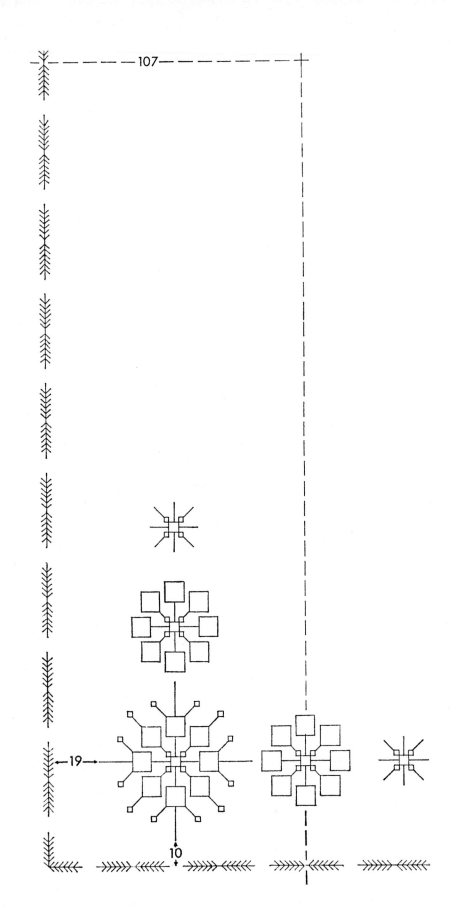

Tablecloth—*Almeria*

Materials

Clarks ⚓ Anchor Stranded Cotton: 8 skeins Black **0403**. Use 3 strands for main embroidery, 2 strands for whipping of Back stitch outlines, or;

Clarks ⚓ Anchor Pearl Cotton No. 8 (10 (gram ball): 2 balls Black **0403**.

2 yd (1 m 82·8 cm) ivory or white fine evenweave fabric, as in illustration, 52 in. (131·8 cm) wide, 28 threads to 1 in. (2·5 cm).

1 Milward 'Gold Seal' tapestry needle No. 24.

The finished size of the cloth is $69\frac{1}{2}$ in. × $49\frac{1}{2}$ in. (176·4 cm × 125·5 cm)

Suitable fabric: *Glenshee* evenweave linen (Ivory).

Instructions

Mark the centre of fabric both ways with a line of basting stitches. The diagram gives one-quarter of the design, centre marked by arrows which should coincide with the basting stitches. The diagram also shows the arrangement of the stitches on the threads of the fabric represented by the background lines. Follow the diagram and number key for the design and stitches used. Commence centrally on lengthwise basting stitches and work the section given. Work in reverse from centres to complete the other three quarters. Repeat the design once more on each lengthwise side of central design spacing 3 in. (7·5 cm) apart. All stitches are worked over 3 threads of fabric. See page 23 for method of working the stitches. Finish with 1 in. (2·5 cm) hem.

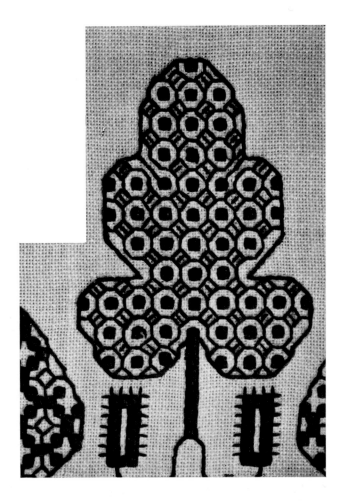

1 Back Stitch
2 Whipped Back Stitch
3 Cross Stitch
4 Straight Stitch
5 Back Stitch (Rose Pattern)
6 Ringed Back Stitch Pattern

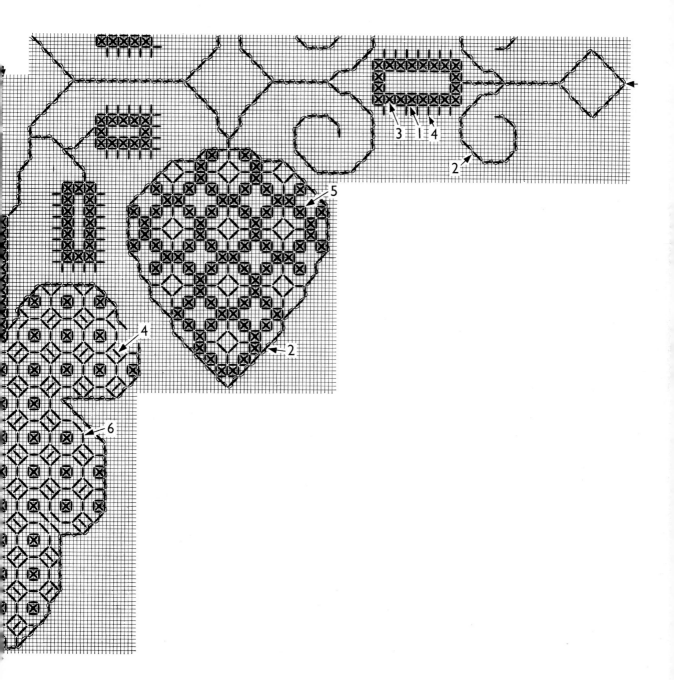

Luncheon mats

Materials

Clarks ⚓ Anchor Pearl Cotton No. 5 (25 metre skein): 2 skeins White **0402** and 1 skein Black **0403**, or;

Clarks ⚓ Anchor Stranded Cotton: 7 skeins White **0402** and 4 skeins Black **0403**. Use 6 strands throughout.

½ yd (45·7 cm) scarlet medium weight square weave cotton fabric, 45 in. (114·3 cm) wide 8–9 squares to 1 in. (2·5 cm).

1 Milward 'Gold Seal' tapestry needle No. 20.

The finished size of each mat is 16 in. × 12 in. (40·6 cm × 30·5 cm)

Suitable fabric: *Panamette* (Scarlet).

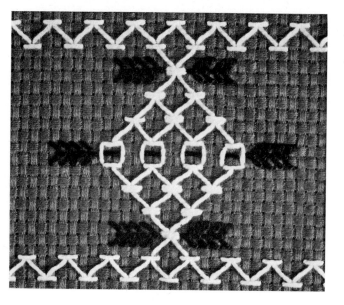

Instructions

Cut three pieces from fabric 18 in. × 15 in. (45·7 cm × 38 cm). Mark the centre both ways on each piece with a line of basting stitches. The diagram gives half the design, centre marked by blank arrow which should coincide with the lengthwise basting stitches. The diagram also shows the arrangement of the stitches on the squares of the fabric represented by the double background lines. With one narrow end facing, commence the design centrally on each piece of fabric 32 squares up from the crossed basting stitches and work the section given, repeat in reverse to complete one side. Turn fabric and work the design at the opposite end in the same way Follow the diagram and number key for the design and stitches used. See pages 19 and 23 for making up of articles and method of working the stitches. Press embroidery on the wrong side. Trim margins even. Turn back ½ in. (1·3 cm) hems on all mats, mitre the corners and slipstitch.

1—**0402** ⎱
2—**0403** ⎰ *Straight Stitch*
3—**0402**—*Chevron Stitch*
4—**0403**—*Fly Stitch*

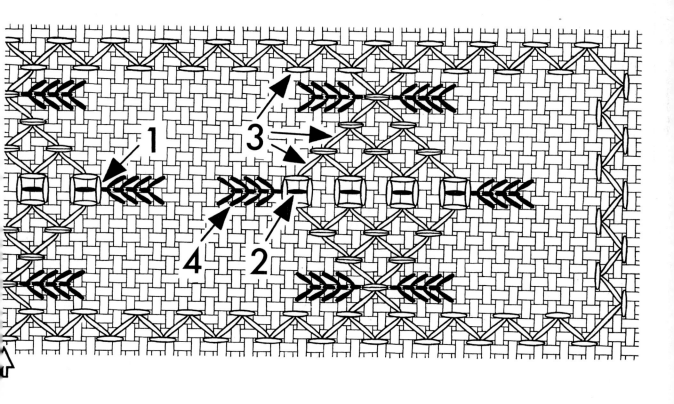

Runner

Materials

Clarks ⚓ Anchor Stranded Cotton: 5 skeins
Black **0403**; 2 skeins White **0402**; 1 skein
Parrot Green **0255**. Use 3 strands through-
out.

½ yd (45·7 cm) jade medium weight evenweave fabric, as in close-up approximately
25 threads to 1 in. (2·5 cm), 50 in.
(126·8 cm) wide.

1 Milward 'Gold Seal' tapestry needle No. 24.

The finished size of runner is approximately
45 in. × 14 in. (114·3 cm × 35·5 cm).

Suitable fabric: *Glenshee* evenweave linen
SP Quality (Jade).

⊡ — 0255

⊡ — 0402

⊡ — 0403

Instructions

Mark the centre of fabric both ways with a line of basting stitches. The Cross stitch is worked over 3 threads of fabric, approximately 8 crosses to 1 in. (2·5 cm). The diagram gives a section of the design, centre marked by blank arrows which should coincide with the basting stitches. Each background square of the diagram represents 3 threads of fabric. With one long side of fabric facing commence the design 3 threads to the left of crossed basting stitches and work the given section, following the diagram and sign key for the embroidery. Work the given section once more to the left leaving no space between. To complete, work the right-hand side to correspond. Press embroidery on the wrong side.

Trim fabric to within 3¾ in (9·4 cm) of embroidery at each long side, measuring from outer white cross stitches and 4¾ in. (12 cm) at short sides. Make up runner taking ½ in. (1·3 cm) hems.

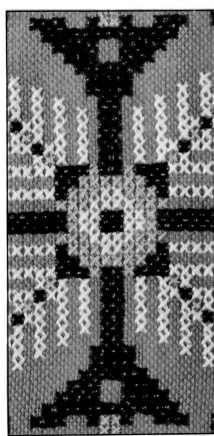

Harvest Table Runners

Materials

Clark's ⚓ Anchor Stranded Cotton: 1 skein each Geranium **010, 013,** Turkey Red **047,** Raspberry **068, 069, 072,** Cyclamen **087, 089,** Violet **0100, 0102,** Parma Violet **0110,** Laurel Green **0206, 0210, 0212,** Moss Green **0267, 0269,** Muscat Green **0279,** Amber Gold **0305, 0306, 0307,** Flame **0335,** Oak Brown **0357** and White **0402.** Use 3 strands throughout.

1 yd (91·4 cm) white medium weight even-weave fabric, as in illustration, 21 threads to 1 in. (2·5 cm), 59 in. (149·7 cm) wide.

1 Milward 'Gold Seal' tapestry needle No. 24.

The finished size of each illustrated runner is 15 in. × 57½ in. (54·6 cm × 146 cm).

Suitable fabric: *Penelope* evenweave linen K302 (White).

Instructions

Cut two pieces from fabric 16½ in. × 59 in. (42 cm × 149·7 cm). Mark each piece across the centre both ways with a line of basting stitches. The design is worked throughout in Cross stitch over two threads of fabric approximately 10 stitches to 1 in. (2·5 cm). The diagram gives one section of the design; each background square represents two threads of fabric. With long side of each piece facing, commence the embroidery at black arrow 4 in. (10 cm) up from crossed basting stitches and 17 threads to the left. Work section given following the diagram and sign key. Repeat section 10 threads to the left omitting extreme left-hand motif. Work section twice more to the right, omitting extreme right-hand motif. Press the embroidery on the wrong side. Make up, taking ½ in. (1·3 cm) hems.

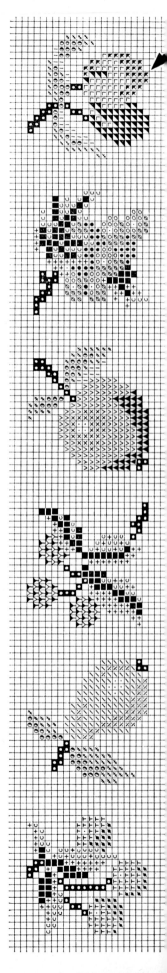

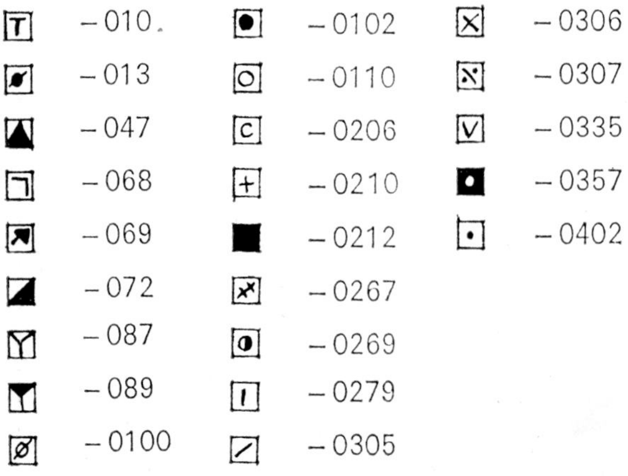

Symbol	Colour	Symbol	Colour	Symbol	Colour
T	– 010	◉	– 0102	✕	– 0306
⬕	– 013	O	– 0110	⊠	– 0307
▲	– 047	C	– 0206	V	– 0335
�	– 068	+	– 0210	◨	– 0357
⬈	– 069	■	– 0212	·	– 0402
◣	– 072	⋈	– 0267		
Y	– 087	◑	– 0269		
ⵊ	– 089	I	– 0279		
⃠	– 0100	╱	– 0305		

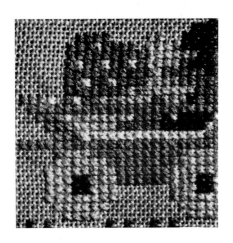

Tablecloth

Materials

Clarks ⚓ Anchor Stranded Cotton: 2 skeins each White **0402**, Special **0850**; 1 skein Tapestry Shade **0851**. Use 4 strands throughout.

1⅝ yd (1 m 48 cm) pale blue medium weight evenweave fabric, as in illustration, 21 threads to 1 in. (2·5 cm), 59 in. (149·7 cm wide.

1 Milward 'Gold Seal' tapestry needle No. 24.

The finished size of the tablecloth is approximately 56 in. (142 cm) square.

Suitable fabric: *Penelope* evenweave linen K303 shade No. 19 (Ice Blue).

Instructions

Square the fabric and mark the centre both ways with a line of basting stitches—these lines act as a guide when placing the design. The diagram gives a section of the design, centre indicated by blank arrows, which should coincide with the basting stitches. The diagram also shows the arrangement of the stitches on the threads of the fabric, represented by the background lines. Follow diagram and number key for the design and stitches used. Each stitch of the Reversed Faggot Filling must be pulled firmly. Commence embroidery centrally with Satin stitch one thread from crossed basting stitches and work the section given. Repeat in reverse on to left-hand side of basting stitches to complete one-quarter of the design. Turn fabric and repeat on to other three lines of basting stitches, completing centre motif. Press the embroidery on the wrong side. Turn back 1 in. (2·5 cm) hem, mitre corners and baste. Work Pin stitch over 2 threads to secure hem edge.

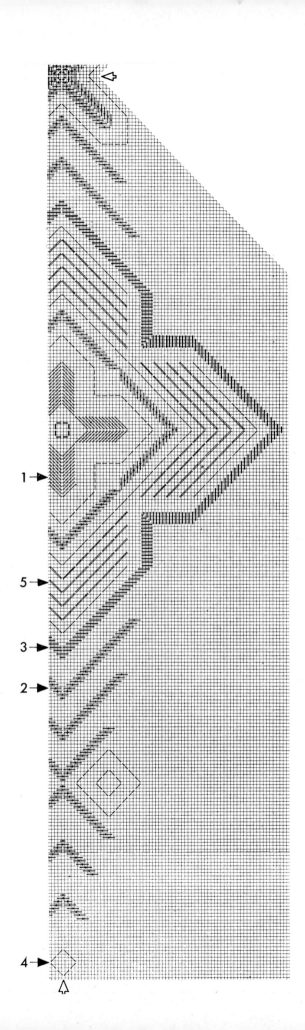

1 →

5 →

3 →

2 →

4 →

1—0402 ⎤
2—0850 ⎬ Satin Stitch
3—0851 ⎦
4—0402—Back Stitch
5—0402—Reverse Faggot Stitch
Filling

Tablecloth

Materials

Clarks ⚓ Anchor Stranded Cotton: 4 skeins Rose Madder **057**; 3 skeins each Rose Madder **055**, Periwinkle **0119**, Apple Green **0203**, Forest Green **0216**; 2 skeins each Cyclamen **087**, Electric Blue **0142** and Kingfisher **0160**. Use 4 strands throughout.

1⅝ yd (1 m 48·5 cm) white medium weight evenweave fabric, as in illustration, approximately 21 threads to 1 in. (2·5 cm), 59 in. (149·7 cm) or 54 in. (137 cm) wide.

1 Milward 'Gold Seal' tapestry needle No. 24.

The finished size of the tablecloth is approximately 56 in. (142 cm) square from 59 in. (149·7 cm) wide fabric or 51 in. (129·3 cm) square from 54 in. (137 cm) wide fabric.

Suitable fabrics: *Penelope* evenweave linen K302 (White). *Beau-Lin* evenweave linen (White).

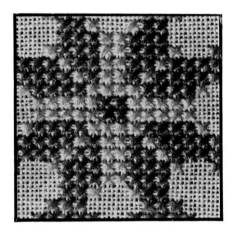

Instructions

Square fabric and mark the centre both ways with a line of basting stitches. The Cross stitch is worked over 3 threads of fabric, approximately 7 crosses to 1 in. (2·5 cm). The diagram gives quarter of the design, centre marked by blank arrows which should coincide with the basting stitches. Each background square of the diagram represents 3 threads of fabric. Commence the design at small black arrow 114 threads to the left of crossed basting stitches and work the given quarter, following the diagram and sign key for the embroidery. To complete, turn fabric and work other three quarters in the same way. (*Note—It is important that the upper stitches of all crosses should lie in the same direction*) Press embroidery on the wrong side. Make up tablecloth taking 1 in. (2·5 cm) hems.

Traycloth

Materials

Clarks ⚓ Anchor Stranded Cotton: 4 skeins Black **0403**; 2 skeins each Nasturtium **0328, 0330**, Flame **0334** and White **0402**. Use 6 strands throughout.

½ yd (45·7 cm) white or natural medium weight evenweave linen, as in illustration, 59 in. (149·7 cm) or 54 in. (137 cm) wide 21 threads to 1in. (2·5 cm) (sufficient for 2 traycloths).

1 Milward 'Gold Seal' tapestry needle No. 20.

The finished size of the traycloth is 14 in. × 20 in. (35·5 cm × 50·7 cm). The cut size is 15½ in. × 21½ in. (39·4 cm × 54·6 cm).

Suitable fabrics: *Penelope* evenweave linen K302 (White). *Beau-Lin* evenweave linen (Natural).

Instructions

Cut one piece from fabric 15½ in. × 21½ in. (39·4 cm × 54·6 cm). Mark the centre both ways with a line of basting stitches. The Florentine stitch is worked throughout over 4 threads of the fabric. The diagram gives a section of the design, centre marked by blank arrow which should coincide with the basting stitches. The background lines of the diagram represent the threads of the fabric. Follow the diagram and sign key for the embroidery. With one long side facing, commence at blank arrow 62 threads down from crossed basting stitches and work section given. Repeat section within brackets twice to the right. Work left-hand side to correspond. Turn fabric and repeat on other long side. With one short side facing work section three times 124 threads down from crossed basting stitches. Repeat on other short side to complete design. Press the embroidery on the wrong side. Trim margins even. Turn back ½ in. (1·3 cm) hems, mitre corners and slipstitch.

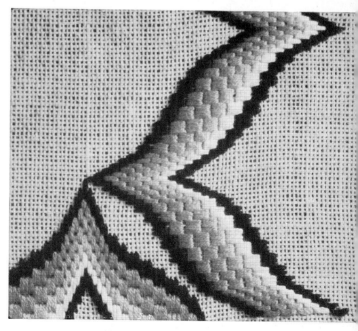

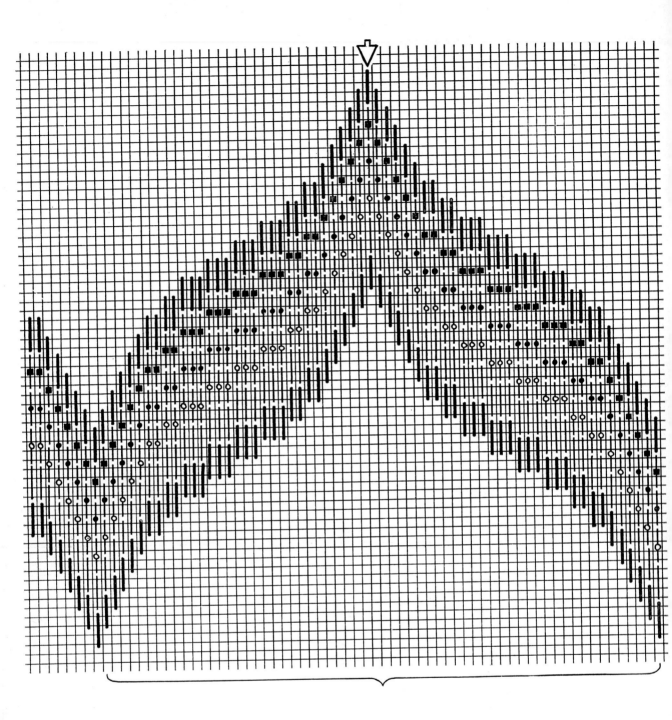

0328
0330
0334
0402
0403

○ — 0186

⊡ — 0188

⊠ — 0117

◩ — 0123

☒ — 0402

Traycloth

Materials

Clarks ⚓ Anchor Stranded Cotton: 3 skeins Cobalt Blue **0133**; 2 skeins Muscat Green **0279** and 1 skein Jade **0187**. Use 3 strands for Jade and 6 strands for remainder of embroidery.

½ yd (45·7 cm) cream medium weight square weave cotton fabric, as in illustration, 45 in. (114·3 cm) wide, 9 squares to 1 in. (2·5 cm).

1 each Milward 'Gold Seal' tapestry needles Nos. 20 and 24 (6 and 3 strands respectively).

The finished size of the traycloth is 14 in. × 20 in. (35·5 cm × 50·7 cm)

Suitable fabric: *Panamette* (Cream).

Instructions

Cut a piece from the fabric 18 in. × 22½ in· (45·7 cm × 57 cm) and mark the centre both ways with a line of basting stitches. The diagram gives a quarter of the design, centres marked by blank arrows which should coincide with the basting stitches. The diagram also shows the arrangement of the stitches on the squares of the fabric represented by the double background lines. Follow diagram and number key for the embroidery. With one long side facing, commence the design on top left-hand quarter at black arrows, 43 squares from the crossed basting stitches, repeat in reverse on lower quarter. To complete, turn fabric and work other half in same way. Press the embroidery on the wrong side. Trim margins even. Turn back ½ in. (1·3 cm) hems, mitre the corners and slipstitch.

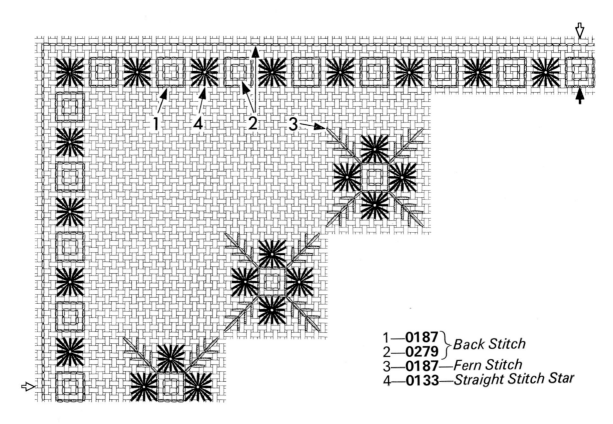

1—**0187** ⎱ *Back Stitch*
2—**0279** ⎰
3—**0187**—*Fern Stitch*
4—**0133**—*Straight Stitch Star*

Traycloth

Materials

Clarks ⚓ Anchor Stranded Cotton: 2 skeins each Jade **0188**, White **0402**; 1 skein each Periwinkle **0117**, Delphinium **0123** and Jade **0186**. Use 3 strands throughout.

½ yd (45·7 cm) red medium weight evenweave fabric, as in illustration, approximately 21 threads to 1 in. (2·5 cm), 59 in. (149·7 cm) or 54 in. (137 cm) wide.

1 Milward 'Gold Seal' tapestry needle No. 24.

The finished size of the traycloth is approximately 21 in. × 14 in. (53·3 cm × 35·5 cm)

Suitable fabrics: *Penelope* evenweave linen K303 shade No. 50 (Procion Red). *Beau-Lin* vat dyed evenweave linen (Red).

Instructions

Cut a piece from fabric 25 in. × 18 in. (63·4 cm × 45·7 cm). Mark the centre both ways with a line of basting stitches. The Cross stitch is worked over 2 threads of fabric. approximately 11 crosses to 1 in. (2·5 cm). The diagram gives a little more than quarter of the design, centre marked by blank arrows which should coincide with the basting stitches. Each background square of the diagram represents 2 threads of fabric. With one long side of fabric facing commence the design 1 thread down and 5 threads to the left of crossed basting stitches and work the given quarter, following the diagram and sign key for the embroidery. To complete, work other three quarters to correspond. Press embroidery on the wrong side. Trim fabric to within 1½ in. (3·8 cm) of embroidery. Make up traycloth taking ½ in. (1·3 cm) hems.

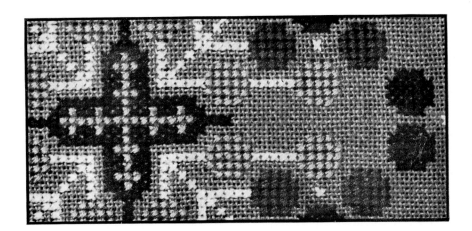

Trolley Set

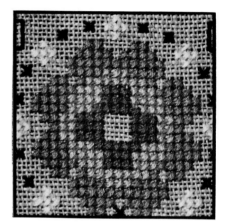

Materials
for two trolley cloths

Clarks ⚓ Anchor Stranded Cotton: 6 skeins Cyclamen **086**; 4 skeins Black **0403**; 3 skeins each Geranium **011**, Magenta **065** and White **0402**. Use 3 strands throughout.

½ yd (45·7 cm) light blue medium weight evenweave fabric, as in illustration, approximately 21 threads to 1 in. (2·5 cm), 59 in. (149·7 cm) or 54 in. (137 cm) wide.

1 Milward 'Gold Seal' tapestry needle No. 24.

The finished size of each cloth is approximately 24 in. × 16 in. (61 cm × 40·6 cm)

Suitable fabrics: *Penelope* evenweave linen K303 No. 8 (Blue). *Beau-Lin* vat-dyed evenweave linen (Blue).

Instructions

Cut two pieces from fabric 26 in. × 18 in. (66 cm × 45·7 cm). Mark the centre of each piece of fabric both ways with a line of basting stitches. The embroidery stitches are worked over 2 threads of fabric, approximately 11 Cross stitches to 1 in. (2·5 cm). The diagram gives a little more than quarter of the design, centre marked by blank arrows which should coincide with the basting stitches. Each background square of the diagram represents 2 threads of fabric. With one long side of fabric facing commence the design 2 threads down and 29 threads to the left of crossed basting stitches and work the given quarter, following the diagram and sign key for the embroidery. To complete, work other three quarters to correspond. Press embroidery on the wrong side.

Trim fabric to within 1½ in. (3·8 cm) of embroidery. Make up trolley cloths taking ½ in. (1·3 cm).

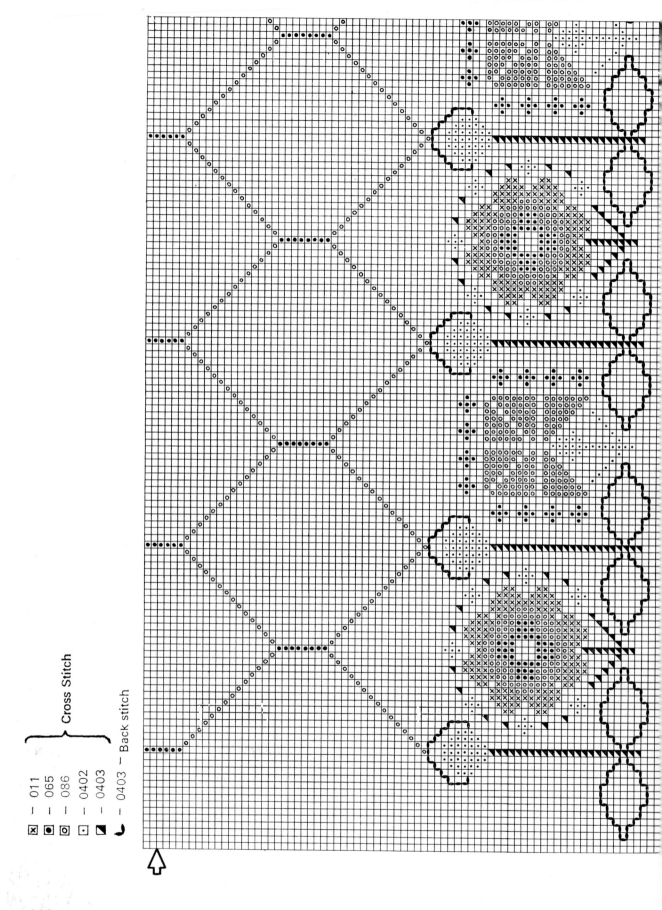

Cross Stitch

⊠ – 011
● – 065
⊙ – 086
· – 0402
◣ – 0403
↻ – 0403 – Back stitch

108

Christmas
Trolley Set

Christmas Trolley Set

Materials

Clarks ⚓ Anchor Stranded Cotton: 5 skeins Amber Gold **0306**; 1 skein each Geranium **08**, Carmine Rose **045**, Scarlet **046**, Violet **0101**, Parma Violet **0108**, Saxe Blue **0150**, Jade **0187**, Orange **0324**, Cinnamon **0370**, Grey **0398**, and White **0402**. Use 3 strands throughout.

¾ yd (68·5 cm) dark blue evenweave fabric, as in illustration, 25 threads to 1 in. (2·5 cm), 50 in. (126·8 cm) wide.

1 Milward 'Gold Seal' tapestry needle No. 24.

The finished size of each illustrated trolley cloth is 16 in. × 24 in. (40·6 cm × 61 cm)

Suitable fabric: *Glenshee* evenweave linen, SP quality (Royal Blue).

Instructions

Cut two pieces from fabric 18 in. × 26 in. (45·7 cm × 66 cm). Mark the centre both ways with a line of basting stitches. The design is worked throughout in Cross stitch over 3 threads of fabric—approximately 8 stitches to 1 in. (2·5 cm). The diagram gives lower right-hand section of the design (A), centres indicated by blank arrows which should coincide with the basting stitches and also gives one small motif (B). Each background square on the diagram represents 3 threads of fabric. With long side of one piece facing, commence the embroidery at black arrow 30 threads down and 42 threads to the right of crossed basting stitches and work section A as given following the diagram and sign key.

To complete border, work other three quarters to correspond. Work small motif (B) in top left-hand corner 42 threads from border. On other piece of fabric, work border and small motif in same way. Repeat small motif in other three corners. Press the embroidery on the wrong side. Trim fabric to within 1¼ in. (3·2 cm) from embroidery on all sides. Make up, taking ½ in. (1·3 cm) hems.

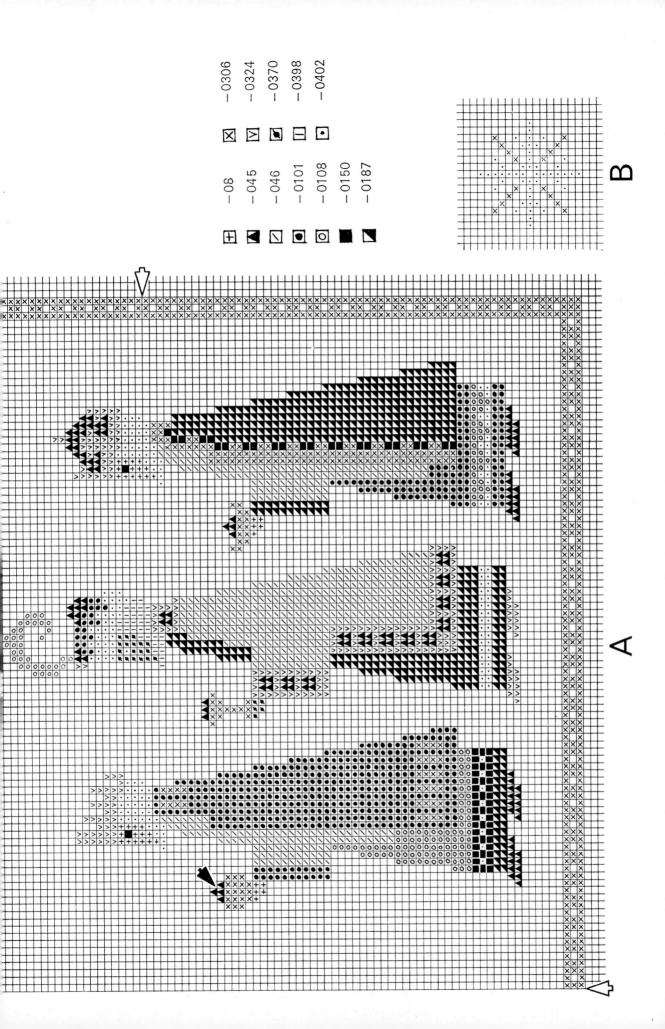

⊠	— 08	— 0306
◩	— 045	— 0324
◪	— 046	— 0370
⊡	— 0101	— 0398
⊙	— 0108	— 0402
⊞	— 0150	
◣	— 0187	

A

B

Trolley Cloths

Materials

Clarks ⚓ Anchor Pearl Cotton No. 8 (10 gram ball): 3 balls Linen **0392**.

½ yd (45·7 cm) pale blue medium weight evenweave fabric, as in illustration, 21 threads to 1 in. (2·5 cm), 59 in. (149·7 cm) wide.

1 Milward 'Gold Seal' tapestry needle No. 24.

The approximate finished size of each cloth is 15 in. × 24 in. (38 cm × 61 cm)

Suitable fabric: *Penelope* evenweave linen K303 shade No. 19 (Ice Blue).

Instructions

Cut two pieces from fabric 18 in. × 27 in. 45·7 cm × 68·5 cm). Mark the centre both ways on each piece of fabric with a line of basting stitches; these lines act as a guide when placing the design. The diagram gives a corner turning and a section of the design, widthwise basting stitches indicated by blank arrow. The diagram also shows the arrangement of the stitches on the threads of the fabric, represented by the background lines. Follow diagram and number key for the design and stitches used. Each stitch must be pulled firmly. With long side of fabric facing,

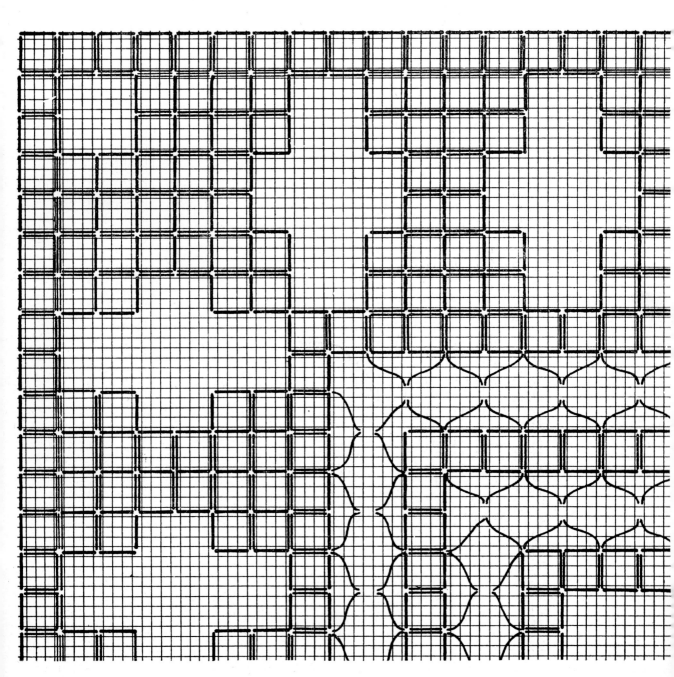

commence the design at the blank arrow 108 threads up from the crossed basting stitches and work section A (Four-sided Wave Filling) only, continue working this section to the left. until there are 52 four-sided stitches on the inside edge, turn corner as shown and continue on short side until there are 28 four-sided stitches including corner stitch; this completes one quarter. Continue in this way until rectangle is formed. Section B is now worked on all sides as shown. To complete design, work section C (Squared edging stitch). Press embroidery on wrong side.

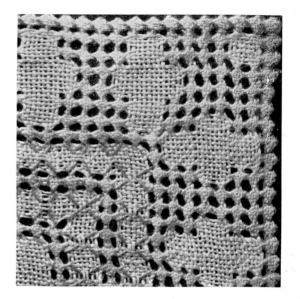

1 Four-sided Wave Filling stitch
2 Four-sided stitch
3 Square Edging stitch

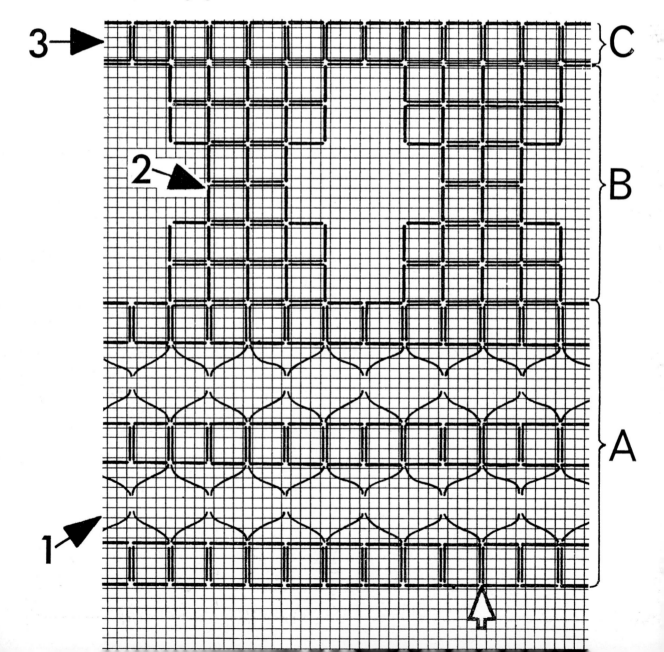

Christmas Wall Hanging

Materials

Coats ⚓ Anchor Tapisserie Wool: 10 skeins **0424**; 3 skeins **0402**; 2 skeins **0185**; 1 skein each **0280, 0311, 0313, 0314, 0325, 0336** and **0375**.

¾ yd (68·5 cm) single thread tapestry canvas, 18 threads to 1 in. (2·5 cm), 27 in. (68·5 cm) wide.

⅜ yd (34·3 cm) orange linen or similar medium weight fabric, 36 in. (91·4 cm) wide, for backing.

1 tapestry fame with 24 in. (61 cm) tapes.

1 wooden rod or cane, 13 in. (33 cm) long and approximately ½ in. (1·3 cm) in diameter.

1 yd (91·4 cm) matching cord, approximately ¼ in. (6 mm) thick.

1 Milward 'Gold Seal' tapestry needle No. 18.

The finished size of the hanging is approximately 22 in. × 10 in. (55·8 cm × 25·4 cm)

Suitable canvas: *Penelope Petit Point* embroidery canvas K099.

Instructions

Mark the centre of canvas both ways with a line of basting stitches. Mount the canvas on the frame—fold down ½ in. (1·3 cm) of the cut edges of canvas and sew securely to the tape on the rollers which lie at the top and bottom of the frame; wind the surplus canvas round the rollers, assemble the frame and adjust the screws so that the canvas is stretched taut from top to bottom. The sides of the canvas are now laced round the laths with fine string or 4 strands of button thread. The diagram gives the complete design, centre indicated by blank arrows which should coincide with the basting stitches. The design is worked throughout in Satin stitch. Each background square on the diagram represents one block of 4 Satin stitches over 4 threads of canvas. Commence the design centrally, following the diagram and sign key for the embroidery.

Making up

Trim canvas to within 2 in. (5 cm) from embroidery at upper edge and 1 in. (2·5 cm) at sides and lower edge. Cut a piece from backing fabric the same size as canvas. Place both pieces right sides together and sew lower edge and two sides close to embroidery to within 4 in. (10 cm) of upper raw edge. To make channel for rod, turn in 1 in. (2·5 cm) canvas margin at the sides of upper edge, then fold over the 2 in. (5 cm) margin and lightly catch stitch the raw edge to wrong side. Turn to right side; turn in remaining seam allowance on backing fabric and slipstitch in position, leaving 1 in. (2·5 cm) at top of sides for insertion of rod. Insert rod. Attach cord at each end of rod.

◪	– 0185
⊠	– 0280
·	– 0311
Ⅰ	– 0313
⊠	– 0314
⊙	– 0325
⊂	– 0336
⬤	– 0375
☐	– 0402
■	– 0424

Child's Wall Hanging

Materials

Coats ⚓ Anchor Tapisserie Wool: 14 skeins or 3 hanks Biscuit **0899**; 6 skeins Flame **0332**; 5 skeins each Gobelin Green **0860**, Smoke **0987**; 4 skeins Tangerine **0315**; 3 skeins each Apple Green **0202**, Moss Green **0266**, Muscat Green **0278**, Biscuit **0905**; 2 skeins each Saxe Blue **0145**, Gobelin Green **0862**, Pink **0892**; 1 skein each Carnation **024**, Cornflower **0139** and Apple Green **0203**.

$\frac{3}{4}$ yd (68·5 cm) double thread tapestry canvas, 10 holes to 1 in. (2·5 cm), 27 in. (68·5 cm) wide.

$\frac{5}{8}$ yd (57 cm) black linen or similar medium weight fabric, 36 in. (91·4 cm) wide, for backing.

1 bamboo rod, approximately 28 in. (71 cm) long and 1 in. (2·5 cm) in diameter.

7 curtain rings, 1$\frac{1}{2}$ in. (3·8 cm) in diameter.

1$\frac{1}{4}$ yd (1 m 14·3 cm) matching cord approximately $\frac{1}{4}$ in. (6 mm) thick or 2 skeins Gobelin Green **0862**; 2 tassels to match cord, approximately 5 in. (12·7 cm) long or 2 skeins Gobelin Green **0862**.

1 Milward 'Gold Seal' tapestry needle No. 18.

The finished size of the illustrated wall hanging is approximately 24 in. × 19 in. (61 cm × 48·2 cm).

Suitable canvas: *Penelope* double thread tapestry canvas, écru, K119.

Instructions

Mark the centre of canvas both ways with a line of basting stitches run from raw edge to raw edge along a line of holes and from selvedge to selvedge between a pair of narrow double threads (see page 13). Mount the canvas as given in the instructions on page 11. The diagram p. 120 gives the complete design, centre indicated by blank arrows which should coincide with the basting stitches. Each background square on the diagram represents one block of 3 double Satin stitches over 3 double threads of canvas. Commence the design centrally and follow the diagram and sign key for the embroidery. When all Satin Stitch has been completed work Straight stitch whiskers in Smoke **0987** as shown in the colour plate.

Making up

Trim canvas to within 1 in. (2·5 cm) from embroidery. Cut a piece from backing fabric the same size as canvas. Place back and front pieces right sides together and stitch to close to the embroidery leaving an opening at the lower edge. Turn to right side. Turn in the seam allowance on the open edges and slip-stitch together. Stitch cord and a tassel in position at each side. Use a 6 in. (15·2 cm) piece of cardboard and 1 skein of wool for each tassel, and four 3$\frac{1}{2}$ yd (3 m 20 cm) lengths of wool for each cord. Stitch curtain rings to top edge. spacing evenly. Insert rod.

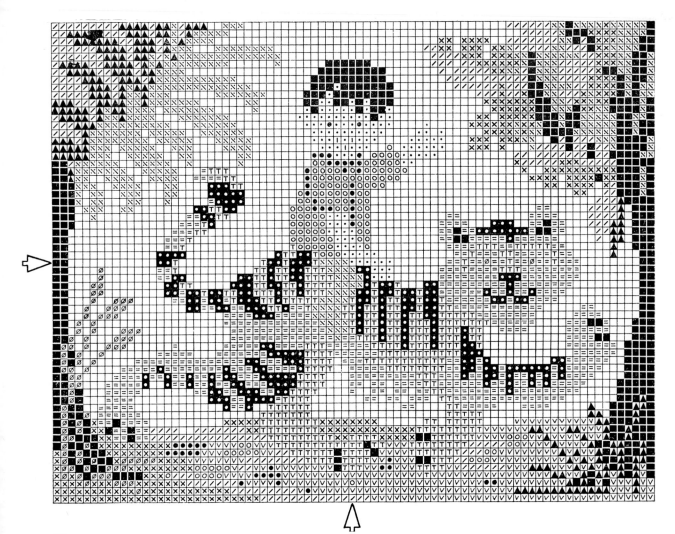

Ⅰ	–	024
●	–	0139
Ⓞ	–	0145
Ⅴ	–	0202
Ø	–	0203
✕	–	0266
╱	–	0278
Ⓣ	–	0315
═	–	0332
◥	–	0860
▲	–	0862
•	–	0892
☐	–	0899
◨	–	0905
■	–	0987

Stool Top

Materials

Clarks ⚓ Anchor Stranded Cotton: 8 skeins Carnation **025**; 7 skeins each Raspberry **069** tapestry shades **0850** and Rose Madder **058**.

Use 6 strands throughout.

$\frac{5}{8}$ yd (57 cm) grey, medium weight even-weave fabric, as in illustration, 20 threads to 1 in. (2·5 cm), 54 in (137 cm) wide.

Stool top 24 in. × 15 in. (60·9 cm × 38 cm) or size required.

1 Milward 'Gold Seal' tapestry needle No. 20.

The finished size of the illustrated stool top is 24 in. × 15 in. (60·9 cm × 38 cm).

Suitable fabric: Beau-Lin vat-dyed even-weave linen (Grey).

1–025
2– 058
3–0850
4–069

Instructions

Cut a piece from fabric 28 in. × 19 in. (71 cm × 48·2 cm). Mark the centre both ways with a line of basting stitches. The diagram gives a section of the design, centre indicated by blank arrows which should concide with the basting stitches. The diagram also shows the arrangement of stitches on the threads of the fabric represented by the background lines. Follow the diagram and number key for the design and colours used.

The design is worked throughout in Satin stitch. With long side of fabric facing, commence the design 27 threads down and 4 to the left of the crossed basting stitches and work the section within the bracket, repeat this section once more to the right then work section given once. Work left-hand side to correspond. Turn fabric and work other half in same way. The length of the design can be adjusted to suit individual requirements. Press embroidery on the wrong side.

Making up

Place embroidery centrally on the stool pad, fold surplus fabric back and secure in position on the underside with upholstery tacks.

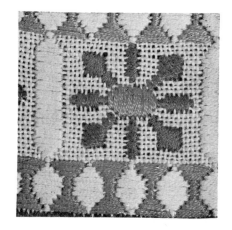

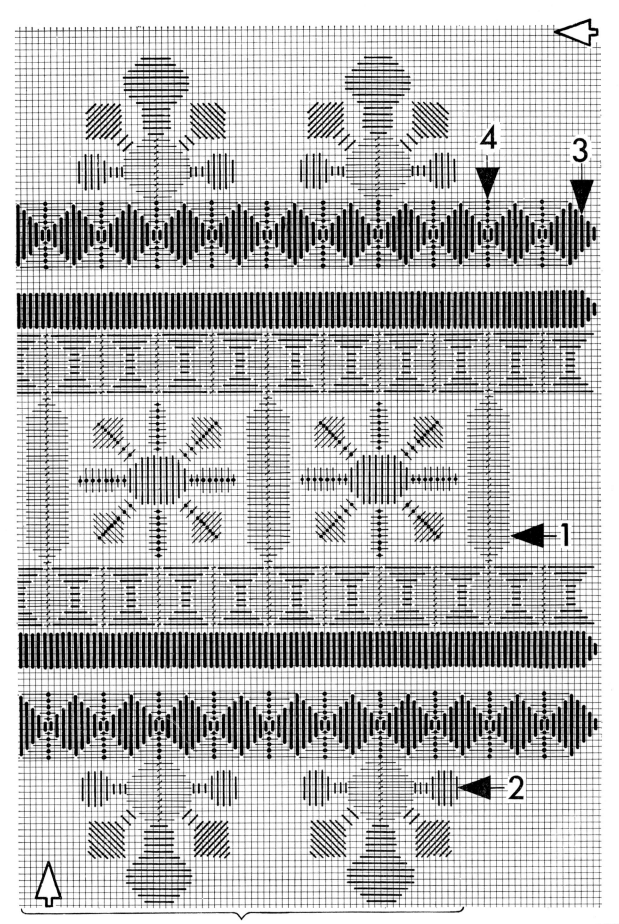

Workbag

Materials

Coats ⚓ Anchor Tapisserie Wool: 31 skeins **0107**; 5 skeins **085**; 3 skeins each **0106** and **0388**.

$1\frac{1}{8}$ yd (1 m 2·7 cm) double thread tapestry canvas, 27 in. (68·5 cm) wide, 10 holes to 1 in. (2·5 cm)

$\frac{1}{2}$ yd (45·7 cm) gold medium weight fabric 36 in. (91·4 cm) wide, for lining.

$\frac{5}{8}$ yd (57 cm) Vilene 32 in. (81·2 cm) wide, for interlining.

1 pair wooden handles with $11\frac{3}{4}$ in. (30 cm) slots.

1 piece cardboard 12 in. × 3 in. (30·5 cm × 7·5 cm) for base.

1 Milward 'Gold Seal' tapestry needle No. 18.

The finished size of the workbag:

Height $12\frac{1}{2}$ in (31·8 cm)
Length at base   12 in. (30·5 cm)
Width at base   3 in. (7·5 cm)
Width at opening   5 in. (12·5 cm)

Suitable canvas: *Penelope* double thread tapestry canvas K119 (Ecru).

Instructions

Mark the centre of canvas both ways with a line of basting stitches run along a line of holes widthwise and between a pair of narrow double threads lengthwise (see page 13). Mount the canvas as given in the instructions on page 11. The diagram gives one half of the design, centre marked by black arrows which should coincide with the basting stitches. Each background square of the diagram represents one block of 3 double Satin stitches, over 3 double threads of canvas. The layout diagram gives one half of the design of the workbag, centres marked by broken lines which should coincide with the basting stitches; the numbers indicate the numbers of Satin stitch blocks. The dotted lines indicate folds and seam lines. Commence the design centrally, following diagram and sign key for the embroidery and work the half given. To complete, work other half to correspond.

To make up

Trim canvas to within 1 in. (2·5 cm) from embroidery on all sides. Using this as a pattern cut one piece each from interlining and lining. Fold embroidered piece in half, wrong side out, matching the horizontal rows of Satin stitches carefully. Stitch side seams as indicated in layout diagram, commencing 1 block in from finished side edge. Fold, so that side seam lies centrally along base section and stitch across base sides. Turn to right side. Make up interlining and lining in same way. Lightly herringbone stitch cardboard in position to interlining. Insert in bag; trim the interlining level with embroidery at gusset edges, sides and fold line at top; turn down seam allowance of canvas on gusset edges over interlining, clip corners and stitch lightly. Turn in sides of section to go through handle slots. Insert lining in bag; trim lining even with interlining at fold line only. Turn down seam allowance level with gusset edges at both sides, clip corners and slipstitch. Turn in seam allowance at sides of handle section and slipstitch then slip handle over embroidered section, fold in half, turn in seam allowance and slipstitch securely.

Work bag

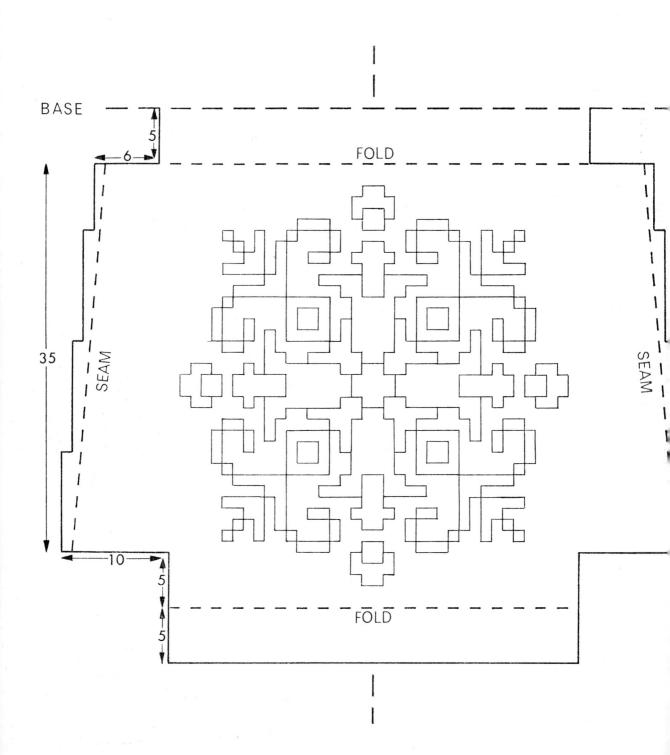

BASE

5

6

FOLD

35

SEAM

SEAM

10

5

5

FOLD

☒ — 085

◉ — 0106

◪ — 0107

⊡ — 0388

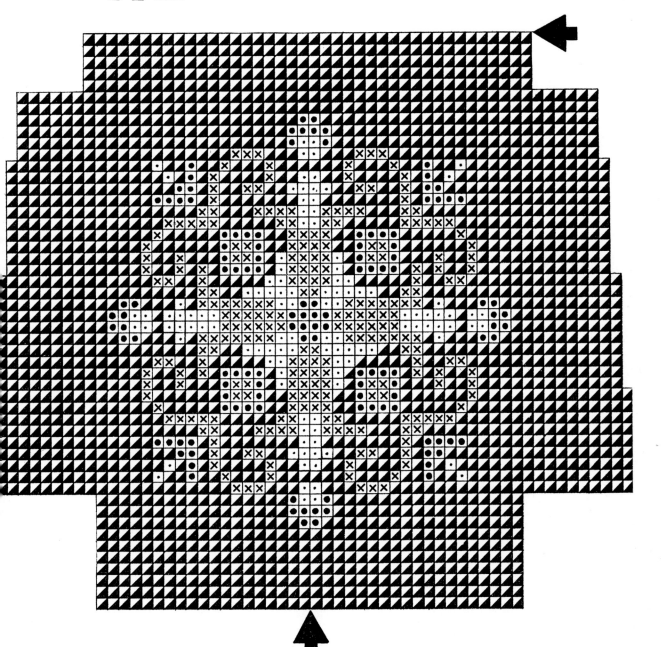